Sex, Lies and Your Soul

Sex, Lies and Your Soul

2nd Edition

Ruth Aj Havbird

Copyright © 2021 by Ruth Aj Havbird.
3rd edition

ISBN: Softcover   978-1-6641-1399-2
               eBook   978-1-6641-1398-5

All rights reserved. No part of this book may be reproduced or transmitted in any form or by any means, electronic or mechanical, including photocopying, recording, or by any information storage and retrieval system, without permission in writing from the copyright owner.

Any people depicted in stock imagery provided by Getty Images are models, and such images are being used for illustrative purposes only.
Certain stock imagery © Getty Images.

Print information available on the last page.

Rev. date: 03/14/2022

To order additional copies of this book, contact:
Xlibris
UK TFN: 0800 0148620 (Toll Free inside the UK)
UK Local: 02036 956328 (+44 20 3695 6328 from outside the UK)
www.Xlibrispublishing.co.uk
Orders@Xlibrispublishing.co.uk
824020

First and fore most, first of all, PLEASE NOTE, that, in this book, I will mention the word vulnerable a lot. I AM NOT SAYING YOU ARE VULNER ABLE BECAUSE YOU ARE A FEMALE, NO I'M NOT SAYING THIS, but simply saying that, one of the things that makes you vulnerable amongst other issues, is if you are a deep sleeper.

Take a sleep test, let someone you trust anyone that you trust, draw on your arm with a washable biro a star or scorpion if you don't wake up soon, this will soon show you that you are a deep sleeper ; and people can molest you if you are around the wrong people so be careful.

Furthermore, I want you to be aware of something, I used to get angry at God for my mishaps/mistakes made in life, bad decisions, though I am now not angry at God for the temptations I face, neither am I saying that God is bad, but I am just trying to make a way of escape if you like out of a difficult situation. Also, trying to make a way to manage temptations as a believer or as an infidel- a non believer of Christ. Remember God is sovereign, and he makes things perfect in his own time.

I will bless the God who gives and takes away.

Also, I'd like to say this, in my own personal opinion, I feel that some witch Drs are reasonable people, meaning that they do what they feel is right for them. I believe that everyone has a freedom of right to express what they believe in, as long as it has nothing to do with harming, others nor me personally or don't try their magic on me.

I may not believe in what they practice, but it is their right to practice it in some countries. However, I want you to note that, I don't believe all witch Drs practice voodoo.

But the ones, <u>alongside ordinary people,</u> who do practice voodoo are harmful and can destroy people's lives. To be honest, I never want to have anything to do with these kind of people, or have any form of contact with such people in my life.

Plus be aware of Blood on the altar of the church, like strange fires like witchcraft and manipulation in the church.

Because, why should a Christian who pays tithes get cancer of any sort, or get fibroid in the site and presence of God? Why are some Christians' bullies for no apparent reason?

If God didn't want you here, that is what he should say pretty please!

I'm not talking about cancer, because that one is a quick death process, sometimes cause by medical negligence, unexplained medical affliction, substantial medical abuse, i.e. abortion.

But, Why do you have to get a slow and painful death of any sort before you leave this world?

Alternatively, why do you have to be under the influence of Aphrodisiac or Viagra, so you could become promiscuous, then if unlucky, may get sexually transmitted disease, then you die in sin, because, …

…[the wages of sin is death, the gift of God is eternal life in Jesus Christ our Lord] KJV Romans 6:24.

That is horrible, those medical doctors are evil. I'm telling you this now!

I reiterate, I repeat, if God didn't want you here, that is what he should say please!

Some medical conditions, are self inflicted,

1. too much sugary stuff, causes diabetics,
2. If you don't take care of yourself, you might get unexplained womb cancer, it is a medical fact. Mysterious Promiscuity might lead to cancer etc. etc.

3. Numerous abortions, in other words more than 5 abortions.
4. The usage of your period, then when it starts to fluctuate in it's flow you develop Fibroid, Adenomyosis; and I am not talking of consistent light flow of blood for predictive times as usual. I.e. if you always get light/ heavy flows for 7 days,
5. Womb removing
6. Using your period
7. Having contraceptives, of all sort, especially the one of cutting fallopian tube, tying of it as well.
8. Sex, Lies, pretence will make you sick indefinitely.

However, do not give all your money to the church, to then be suffering inside, only do what you can afford.

I don't know but some sex drives could be natural or in the worst case scenario, could be the influence of a sexual stimulant. If the devil has tactics, then we ought to have one too. Instead of gallivanting from one man to another man. Why not sleep with your let's say, cousin's man, or husband. If you cannot control your sex drive, until you pray hard and God helps you to be in control of it. [Be sober, be vigilant for the devil your adversary seeketh whom to devour]. Promiscuity could lead to sexually Transmitted disease STD. So be careful. I reiterate that, if your cousin's man or husband is to help you with your sex drive until Mr right comes along, he shouldn't be trapping you in that relationship to get you pregnant, if he does then he is bad also.
Because WHAT IS EVEN IN IT FOR HIM Q?
The safety of our CHILDREN, SHOULD BE THE REASON FOR THE LOVE THAT WE SHARE.
Unless your relative's man, wants to help with your sexual urge, out of kindness, until Mr right comes along. But try to avoid sex before marriage

Then maybe you are BETTER OFF WITH SEX TOYS THEN.

Avoid Escorting as someone there could try to force you to do Anus sex, or even request it, walk off the setting if that is the case. This book is also about, how to prevent and get over an unfruitful relationship, where the man has treated you badly, or have just hurt you. The thing to remember, is that the word of God says in KJV Pro 9:17 "Stolen waters are sweet, and bread eaten in secret is pleasant." Basically, a man that cheats on you might receive the judgement of God so don't worry yourself try to get revenge. Rom 12:2 KJV says also that, 377 "And be not conformed to this world: but be ye transformed by the renewing of your mind, that ye may prove what is that good, and acceptable, and perfect, will of God.

If you want to be a follower of Christ so he can help you to overcome the possibility of Hell fire, also to help you overcome the temptations of this world, then Confess the saviour: Roman 10 : 8-9

Romans 10 :8-9 King James Version (KJV)

10:8 But what saith it? The word is nigh thee, even in thy mouth, and in thy heart: that is, the word of faith, which we preach;

❖ 10:9 That if thou shalt confess with thy mouth the Lord Jesus, and shalt believe in thine heart that God hath raised him from the dead, thou shalt be saved.

1 John 1:9-10 King James Version (KJV)

1:9 If we confess our sins, he is faithful and just to forgive us our sins, and to cleanse us from all unrighteousness.

1:10 If we say that we have not sinned, we make him a liar, and his word is not in us.

King James Version (KJV)

I Peter 5:8 King James Version (KJV)

8 "Be sober, be vigilant; because your adversary the devil, as a roaring lion, walketh about, seeking whom he may devour:" Meaning the devil and evil people are about seeking to take advantage of you, so be vigilant. The devil here is described as a lion, also known as a serpent.

Jesus is described as the lion of a tribe of Judah, so amongst other tribes, he is from the tribe of Juda. Rev 5:5 "And one of the elders saith unto me, Weep not: behold, the Lion of the tribe of Juda, the root of David, hath prevailed to open the book, and to loose the seven seals thereof."

Revelation 21:8 "But the fearful, and unbelieving, and abominable, and murderers, and whoremongers, and sorcerers, and idolaters, and all liar, shall have their part in the lake which burneth fire and brimstone: which is the second death."

You also need to find a bible believing church to get baptised by immersion. Note some preachers worship from home have church at home, so you may need one to book a church baptismal pool, so they can baptise you there, then the church continues at home of the relevant clergy.

KJV Matthew 3:13-17
Matthew 3:13 "Then cometh Jesus from Galilee to Jordan unto John, to be baptized of him."
Matthew 3:14 "But John forbad him, saying, I have need to be baptized of thee, and comest thou to me?"
Matthew 3:15 "And Jesus answering said unto him, Suffer it to be so now: for thus it becometh us to fulfil all righteousness. Then he suffered him."
Matthew 3:16 "And Jesus, when he was baptized, went up straightway out of the water: and, lo, the heavens were opened unto him, and he saw the Spirit of God descending like a dove, and lighting upon him:"
Matthew 3:17 "And lo a voice from heaven, saying, This is my beloved Son, in whom I am well pleased."

KJV Mark 16:15-16
Mark 16:15 "And he said unto them, Go ye into all the world, and preach the gospel to every creature."
Mark 16:16 "He that believeth and is baptized shall be saved; but he that believeth not shall be damned."

John 14:6;26
6 "Jesus saith unto him, I am the way, the truth, and the life: no man cometh unto the Father, but by me."
26 "But the Comforter, which is the Holy Ghost, whom the Father will send in my name, he shall teach you all things, and bring all things to your remembrance, whatsoever I have said unto you."

Fri 12/02/2016 – Fri 11/02/22

I just want to add that here in West Yorkshire, Sat 19.05.2018, during the Royal wedding, I went to learn how to ride a bicycle, though I had plans to keep up with the wedding at some point during the day and I did.

Anyhow, I learnt how to ride a bicycle, it was a fascinating experience, though out of all of the training, I can recall that, in order not to strain your leg, you need to adjust the seat, in such a way that your feet are pointing to the floor, about barely touching the floor. So that after scooting with your comfortable leg which mine is my right leg, I'm righthanded, after scooting with my right leg to then lift of to launch with my right leg, I would not strain that leg when trying to find the pedal to launch on that right pedal. Overall cycling is Great, most especially great for riding in the park with the children, but driving a car is better, since the road is predominantly for vehicles not bicycles.

Take care and God bless, but don't cycle on the road if you don't have the confidence to cycle on the road. However, cycle on the pavement or road wherever you're most comfortable. If you neither want to drive nor learn how to ride a bicycle, that's fine. So then, if a disabled person can drive, so then, if I had to pick 1, I'd rather not ride a bicycle, but I'd rather learn how to drive, than ride a bicycle on the main road. So be careful, I won't say more than that.

I don't mind cycling maybe in the park or something. If you find a man of God that will prophecy to you, then that is good. So then, if the man of God prophecies anything to you from don't go out with a man, you can ignore him and be careful with that man and study him.

Then any bad sign from the man you may dump him quickly, then that will be the prophecy of the man of God coming true. But do not go riding on the main road, or on the pavement, 346 especially not on the main road as you don't need it, I would believe his prophecy, that something bad might happen regarding this type of prophecy. I would go learn how to drive a car instead.

First of all I want to say, deception is not good, so anywhere where I said a married man can first deceive a single woman. Then tell her the truth in due course, is wrong, because I do not know why he has to lie about his marital status.

Men like to lie, plus people in authority encourages lies in our societies, this was why I was giving them room to lie plus tell the truth at the right time, without getting her pregnant of course.

I've come to realise that condoling this kind of behaviour gives room for manipulation. So, I here by openly declare, that if a married man doesn't tell a singlet lady about his marital status in good time, preferably immediately, he will be prosecuted, by a lenient fine, if caught lying to a singlet lady.

<u>Why, not a single man with a girlfriend, but a married man, be so kind, as to come with the intention to help you out with sex,</u> till Mr right comes along, or why can't a male friend or your female relatives man help you with sex if you cannot help needing sex, either way it would be better if you don't need the sex though till Mr right comes along. Why does a married man, have to attempt to propose, secretly to do polygamy this is wrong, in that, they wished it for you, because you didn't wish ....it, they wished it, for you to do polygamy, then you can choose if you want Polygamy, when you find out the truth.

If you decline, then he can stay with his wife, he doesn't need to divorce his wife, when they are supposed to tell the truth.

Also, I'd hope that you keep your virtues o. **O** first and foremost, better still, there should not be any, playing, of games and any time wasting to be deceiving a female. If the man or woman of God, wants to... .....advice a married man to help out a female with her sexual urge, but conceals his marital status for a while as she won't do it if she found out, then when she finds out, the truth at the appropriate time, that he is married, he can go back to his wife he doesn't need to divorce his wife, if she doesn't want to continue with that, but I'm telling you this now, very hardly you will find a married man whose wife would allow this, without there being a catch to get you to do Polygamy, not to talk of a guy with a girlfriend, why do you need sex for in the first place if your Mr right is not there yet. so that when you find out you can be free to dump him. Getting a married man to come and trap you is a lame excuse, because they were undermining your ability to get a single man to yourself so it is not your problem nor is it your fault they should have been thinking with their Godly mind in the first place instead of their devilish mind.

If it wasn't for a sexual stimulant, you wouldn't have been living a promiscuous life though. If some people were not protected by their parents from start, they wouldn't get their Prince by now. Some people has been through hell and back, this is why they are where they are today.

<u>Anything</u> that is not based on the love of God, but is making you conscious of yourself that some strange spirits are in charge of your life, is not from God, they will start to make you hallucinate to be imagining something that's not there, though you won't go mad, but then you could start to go off point. **<u>Like, you might start to have low self-esteem, when thinking something is wrong with you, when thinking something is wrong with you.</u>**

Yes you have a weakness; and God knows why! ! ! ! !-!

Another thing that I am sure of, that will not happen, is that when they get you to hallucinate about a spirit husband/spirit wife, ain't no demonic spirit will be invoked or called down into your life to be spiritually having sex with you in the sleep. I will explain better in a minute. Digressing in relation to this. One thing I do know, is that, demonic oppression, is a spirit that enslaves, but is not necessarily possessing a person.

But people, who are possessed by demons, will be under the influence of demonic demonstration, hence, have probably been a member of **occult** groups before, so be warned that there could be a transference of demonic powers from someone who has been involved in **ocultic** practices to someone who hasn't been involved in occultic practices, in a deliverance room.

So, we need to watch and pray as well plead the blood of Jesus every second of deliverance as appropriate. I think that people who have been involved in the occult are the ones that need deliverance, but not ordinarily church goers, as ordinary church goers need a prophetic utterances from God about their lives as well normal prayer sessions, okay!!!!!!!

You can stay, in a deliverance room separate from those who have been involved in occultic practices. Deliverance, what is that? I still have a lot of love for the Charismatic churches, but some churches their doctrines, I no longer believe in them. Because, do the leaders know why exactly, you are a deep sleeper, otherwise, deliverance, doesn't mean anything to me anymore o!

I find some Pastors Amazing they know themselves as I don't want to be calling names.

Back to my opinion as the spirit of God is leading me to understand, regarding this matter, I am sure what will not happen, is that when they get you to hallucinate about a spirit husband/spirit wife, aint no demonic spirit will be invoked or called down into your life to be spiritually having sex with you in the sleep. I want you to understand something that the words incubus and succubus, both are on the google dictionary for a reason; and this is what I believe to be the reason. The words incubus and succubus, has been wrongly described when saying that a demonic is sleeping with you, which can connote or imply, that the individual is being possessed by a demon, which I don't believe to be true. The Greek interpretation, as a man of God's findings reveals. "Incubus, to lie on top," "Succubus to lie under." Meaning, spirit husband spirit wife.

But, I think your ex, could be the spirit husband who violates you sexually, if he is s o obsessed with you, plus won't let you to go be happy with someone else.

I think there is a natural sexual feeling that people feel when they touch, this is why if you are a virgin, don't let a man touch you inappropriately. But there is a sexual booster; and it's call Aphrodisiac/ Viagra, which is a love potion that can turn you on. I heard one type of Aphrodisiac is called Viagra. I heard this from a young but mature black lady, she looked about 26 years old, who shouted out loud, Viagra in the Lewisham library, back 2001, when I was 19 years old, when I was still attending GWC Redeem, in Catford.

Now today 03/July/2017, at the hour of 06:11 am, I checked on the google web page to see the actual definition of Viagra. So, this is what I found.

Sildenafil Medication Consult a doctor if you have a medical concern. **Sildenafil** sold as the brand name Viagra among others, is a medication used to treat erectile dysfunction and pulmonary arterial hypertension. Its effectiveness for treating sexual dysfunction in women has not been demonstrated. Wikipedia Molar mass: 474.5764 g/mol Biological half-life: 3–4 hours Metabolism: Liver: CYP3A4 (major route), CYP2C9 (minor route) Formula: $C_{22}H_{30}N_6O_4S$ Metabolites: N-desmethylsildenafil (~50% potency for PDE5) ATC code: G04BE03 (WHO) License data : EU EMA: Viagra; US FDA: Sildenafil Feedback Sources include: US FDA, US NLM, DailyMed, Micromedex

Hence, it would be right to say, that, Polygamy is wrong and can become devilish, *if not done by natural interventions, as well, if not done by natural affection, or by the instruction of GOD.* if it is done by the influence of Viagra or the likes of medications like this. If God is Holy, then why are we not holy until we get married to our own husband. This is to say that our body is the temple of the holy spirit and that we should flee fornication. KJV I cor 6:17-20

[Thursday-- 10/02,22-- 13:51 PM] Ruth Aj: I hope the next selfish from the church they want to take inspiration from, that they treat her better than they did to me. I hope she doesn't get the same ill, treatment plus harassment.

Holier than thou Christians.

Digressing, there's no time for a long exploration, but I feel that the prevention of homelessness is better than the cure.

Also, if you have a little change to spare, try to give to a homeless person, even 50 pence is something.

Once upon a time, in my life I had determined to give every homeless person 2 pounds every day I went out, whenever, I came in contact with one.

At odd times I was compelled to give 5 or ten pounds. By the end of the month I had given £50 to a couple of homeless people. It all adds up, **but then, I suddenly realized I cannot change their circumstance unless the government helps them.**

The choice is left for the giver to help or not to help with change or not.

I reinforce, that the prevention of homelessness is better than its cure.

Another dream About 2 weeks from today Sun 25/06/2017, I had a dream that my step niece Lola was getting married somewhere, the location of this place wasn't known to me.

But all my family members were invited but me. I wasn't invited to the wedding in this dream. What was God trying to reveal to me in this dream? As I don't get it. Because I was more confused when I woke up, asking why God will not let me see her husband, I thought it was Martins a guy whom I loved, an ex I broke up with a couple of days ago, before this dream back in Aug 2017.

Also, why is he showing me the wedding for, because I don't get it. Sometimes I feel like God is playing mind games, because if he wants to say something he should just say it. Today's date is Sun 25/06/2017 and I am 35 years old, whilst my niece is about 27 years old.

This dream is a real revelation, in that, if a female is under the captivity of a sexual stimulant like Viagra, to try to get her to be sleeping around, instead to be sleeping around, why don't the loved ones and or the pastors, tell her if she doesn't remain near them to be sleeping with her let us say, her cousin's boyfriend or husband, till she can control the urge, she could catch sexually transmitted disease, if she goes far away, hence could gallivant from man to man. **The cousin's boyfriend is bad if he has a motive to trap her with him against her wish to get her pregnant. What do you need sex for, you are better off with sex toys o, then?** *Nor* **do you need the love of your family member's man until Mr right comes along, because the man in question could get nasty, if there is nothing in it for him o o o-!!!--!!!---6---**

I reiterate that, if your cousin's man or husband is to help you with your sex drive until Mr right comes along, he shouldn't be trapping you in that relationship to get you pregnant, if he does then he is bad also. Then maybe you are better off with sex toys then.

[10/02, 03:44] Ruth Aj:

Isaiah 9:6 [Wonderful, mighty God, Prince of peace, counsellor, mighty God, Emmanuel]

09:50 Am Thu 27.Jan/2022

🏠 🏠 🏠🏠 🏠🏠 🏠

Wednesday 12/January/2022

15:36 PM

First of all, read the scriptures if you wish, plus if you don't understand them, pray for understanding 🙏 from God.

God bless!!!

Isa 9:6 backs up how I see God Almighty and his only begotten son Jesus Christ.

God has been good to me.

KJv I Corinthians 12:25 "That there should be no schism in the body; but that the members should have the same care one for another." 1 Corinthians

even if someone is weak, let the other stronger party support them.

however, if someone's vulnerability will affect you, then this means you both are not compatible, marriage wise.

Kjv 22:3 Proverbs "A prudent man foreseeth the evil, and hideth himself: but the simple pass on, and are punished."

New Living Translation Philippians

 4:13

"For I can do everything through Christ, who gives me strength."

(NIV - New International Version) Proverbs 23:9

"Do not speak to (fools), for they will scorn your prudent words."

kjv Matthew 5:22 "But I say unto you, That whosoever is angry with his brother without a cause shall be in danger of the judgment: and whosoever shall say to his brother, Raca, shall be in danger of the council: (but whosoever shall say, Thou (fool), shall be in danger of hell fire.)"

kJV Matthew 7:21-26

7:21 "Not every one that saith unto me, Lord, Lord, shall enter into the kingdom of heaven; but he that doeth the will of my Father which is in heaven."

Mat 7:22 "Many will say to me in that day, Lord, Lord, have we not prophesied in thy name? and in thy name have cast out devils? and in thy name done many wonderful works?" Mat7:23 "And then will I profess unto them, I never knew you: depart from me, ye that work iniquity." 7:24 Mat "Therefore whosoever heareth these sayings of mine, and doeth them, I will liken him unto a wise man, which built his house upon a rock:" Mat 7:25 "And the rain descended, and the floods came, and the winds blew, and beat upon that house; and it fell not: for it was founded upon a rock." Mat 7:26 "And every one that heareth these sayings of mine, and doeth them not, shall be likened unto a foolish man, which built his house upon the sand:"

Some things in life are a nonsense and the ingredients

If you love someone

You'd not die for them, but You'd take a risk knowing you could lose your life or gain it. 50/50

[The bible says, in kjv Mathew 10:16 be wise as a serpent, be gentle as a dove].

[Mat 11:12 since the day of Johnthe Baptist, the kingdom of God suffereth violence, the violence shall take it by force]

07:21Am Tuesday 23.Nov./2021

Ps, thank God for diSsenTers, THEY ARE SUPPORTERS AS WELL FANs of someone.

07:05Am

Mon 22.Nov/2021

Good morning, ladies and gentlemen, Sirs', Madams', Mas', Ma'ams'

Headlines, Testimony time!

Pls, don't turn a furtive ear, to what I'm about to say, like blaa blaa blaah

The church 🏠🙏 is trying to create a scandal with your name, with the men you've been with.

Like who were they with before you?

WhO were they with when you were together? plus wHo were they with after you'd been been together?

Like murder and blood on the altar of God in the church. It's a scandal

Ps give yourself peace of mind; and know that God is with you, also what I am trying to say is, know the men that you go out with before you go out with them.

First and foremost, the True definitions of
SELFISH, are:-

1. Nonchalant attitude
2. No care for others

I. Bitch= Feminine noun or adjective for nasty, Don't
    use it in church.
II. Bastard = Masculine and feminine noun for all
    children of the devil, non followers of Jesus
    Christ.

I know things will not always be perfect, but
let us try our best, to behave in a coherent,
articulate, logical manner. Either way I know
sometimes, you will be yourself; and do you.
As sometimes, some things in life,...

.... It is. what it is.

"If they didn't want us to eat it why did they make it taste so good?" It's something a lovely little American, mixed race girl said on TV programme, I watched at my sister's house back in I think 2011 Sky TV. I DON'T KNOW ABOUT YOU, BUT I LIKE MY FOOD TO TASTE GOOD.

Another, statement made on TV. You're gonna wish you had a rock of a bottom, by the time I've finished with you. Statement made in same TV programme by a nice mixed race lady. Is it a good statement? WELL I THINK IT's INFORMATIVE.

I think what she is trying to say is that, eat the right food, so you won't be constipated. OR ARE THEY TRYING TO MESS ABOUT WITH MEDICATION as usual?

We've all heard the saying, if you cannot beat them, join them. Well I'm telling you now, if you cannot beat them, leave them alone O. Don't join them o! Two wrongs don't make a right O!

The following is to say, please watch your mouth, try to avoid placing curses on those who have hurt you and have despitefully used you. Let God fight for you.

Exodus 14: 14 "The LORD shall fight for you, and ye shall hold your peace."

James 3:10 *Out of the same mouth proceedeth blessing and cursing. My brethren, these things ought not so to be. James 3:11 Doth a fountain send forth at the same place sweet water and bitter?*

James 3:12 *Can the fig tree, my brethren, bear olive berries? Either a vine, figs? so can no fountain both yield salt water and fresh.*

The following is to also say, charity begins at home.

<u>**1 Timothy 5:8** *But if any provide not for his own, and especially for those of his own house, he hath denied the faith, and is worse than an infidel.*</u>

The family you come from are responsible for your care then if you find love, that man and his family take over. This is why you need God more than ever, because true love is hard to find. Why can't people help to nurture your gifts and to help you improve than to always be putting up barriers and focusing on your weaknesses.

May I ask a question, would it be right to rape a physical disabled person, because he/she are disabled or not to do so? Then why should it be right to rape a vulnerable person. So therefore, if your ex is caught trying to rape you, being a vulnerable person, he will be prosecuted for attempted rape.

In the actual sense, if your family members, were to tell you that you were a deep sleeper in the first place; and to tell you that them and the police and any other powerful organisations don't want you to have a baby in real life, though you want children; and it would be nice if they told you not after one child, then we'd get the point faster.

WHY DOES YOUR EX HAVE TO RAPE YOU IN THE SLEEP TO PROVE A DAMN POINT THIS IS VIOLATION; and if caught should be locked up in prison. <u>You better not be sedated with antipsychotics, THAT YOU ARE FORCED TO TAKE WHILST AWAKE</u> either!!!

It is a wicked world in that people would rather make fun of you than to find a more amicable way out of the situation. The family you come from are responsible for your care then if you find love, that man and his family takes over. This is why you need God more than ever because true love is hard to find. Why cannot people help to nurture your gifts and to help you improve than to always be putting up barriers and focusing on your weaknesses.

Digressing, I just want people to know that ever since I attended a college at west Yorkshire, and told one of the Tutors in a group discussion about a relating topic that I once found a piece of blue plastic bag in food. It was as if I was being punished for actually trying to bring it to his attention for him to possibly learn from it and maybe can do something to prevent such in the future, him being a person who knows the food industry well.

But ever since then, in the last two months, this enlightenment for their help, has come back to haunt me instead, I once went to (**not a Thai** restaurant) but **a Chinese Restaurant** @ west Yorkshire; and found a piece of **scouring** wire in my food. Then I bought sandwiched from a West Yorkshire café; and the same blue food bag, a piece of it was found in my sandwich. So, I am just warning people to be careful to watch what they are about to eat in any Restaurant, be it McDonalds or anywhere. Today's date is Thursday 10/05/2018. I am not trying to be funny, I'm just keeping it real.

Note, Since you've prayed, fasted and worshiped God, still the urge doesn't go away. Then, if it is the case that you have no man that you are actually interested in, to have to yourself. **DO NOT GET a male sex worker to have sex with him,** *to be paying him, till you find the right man then, this is wrong, but the choice is yours.*

ARE YOU ON VIAGRA OR APHRODISIAC?

I repeat plus reiterate, that both Male as well Female prostitution, are both a sin!!! I ask again, *ARE YOU ON VIAGRA OR APHRODISIAC?*

If a man were to be divorce and single, or never been married before and single, he can get involved in can get involved in…

…….POLY-A-MORY relationship, that would be his choice, but note this is wrong I don't like it. **WHY CAN'T THE SINGLE FEMALES, GO FOR SOMEONE** who is actually available, or might even be a younger person than them, please?

Why does a married man have to be sleeping with side females, then they *pay the married man, an affordable fee!*

That is indirect male *prostitution isn't it? A married man who is having numerous girlfriends, plus concubines, will not be able to look after his wife properly, nor care for if it is, the case, his only wife. Because of his other MISSES.*

If you, the only main wife at the time finds out, if you wish, you may tell him, to go pick one of his loose women, or O's, to make as a new main wife, Then as usual, to continue with the rest of his side chicks, we'll see how that other new wife, will like that. Treat unto others as you'd like for yourself.

Furthermore, *him doing this is cheating on his wife.*

Then one of his loose women could seduce him to leave the main wife. So A No No to this arrangement please!

Digressing, be warned.

I like my perfume to smell nice, but there is a difference, between nice perfume and such thing as seducing perfume. Be warned.

Hence, so, don't go to a female's home alone. Vice versa, don't go to a male's home alone. Unless you are either going to be faithful if he/she tries to seduce you, **OR ONLY Go ALONE,** if you trust that he / she won't try to seduce you.

It's like, are you kidding me right now? I repeat, what are those single women doing with the married man in the first place. Cannot they find their own man, even a younger person. ARE THEY ON APHRODISIAC OR VIAGRA? Because they don't want to be in control of their sexual urge, are they on Viagra, go marry an available person, even if younger than you, if not SORRY, you cannot SHARE a married man unless you are, ALL plus NO MORE THAN, THE second WIFE, PLUS ALL CONSENTING ADULTS HAVE TO CONSENT, PERIOD!!!

I'm telling you, trying different women will mess that man up, he won't be able to focus on his main wife, if it is his only wife, she might even die from the stress of neglect in the relationship. It is not his responsibility, to be sexing other women, they need their own man o, whatever it takes, even a younger person, so be it! Leave happy married couples alone please.

When a man is married, the law says that he can have girlfriends if he wants.

I don't even know why that is allowed, but Polygamy <u>with the maximum of 2 females,</u> is Illegal.

But Polygamy with the <u>maximum of 2 females,</u> is Illegal

The problem with a married man being allowed to have girlfriend(s) as opposed to polygamy, is that in that type of relationship, the female could leave and ruin the relationship of the man and his wife.

However, I prefer polygamy with a close relative than family friend or than even a good stranger, plus, with all adult participants, consenting.

At least in a polygamous relationship, there is commitment, Plus loyalty. I don't like either of the two, but if you are going to be doing all that, then Polygamy is way better. I don't even think Polygamy is a sin, I just don't like the problem that comes with it...

.......So best do it with a close relative only, not even a so called nice stranger, or family friend. With all consenting parties to actually consent to the act. Anything outside this box, is violation.

If either or both the married man and the new proposed <u>female</u> partner, is or are caught lying to the main wife. The man or both should be prosecuted with lenient fines, or even locked up in Jail, if either or both are caught lying to the main wife, because they can harm with their lies.

As SHE NEEDS TO BE AWARE OF WHAT EXACTLY, HER MAN IS GETTING UP TO.

<u>Wifey,</u> IF YOU CATCH YOUR MAN LYING AND CHEATING, IF HE WON'T LEAVE THAT SELFISH home wrecker ALONE. First of all, stay in the marriage but don't allow him touch you anymore. With prayers, that hopefully he will come to his senses; and leave those loose and selfish, females alone. However, if he forcefully kicks you out of the matrimonial home, and not responding to your kind and patient gestures, as well secret prayers, even if you shout out when he is in the other room, that is still your secret prayers. As you may become, prayerfully, aggressive, when distressed. <u>SO THEN,</u> if he forcefully kicks you out of the matrimonial home, you may want to consider divorcing him. l
Then, MAYBE YOU SHOULD LEAVE THEM TO IT THEN. Go for someone who is available, or that might, even be a younger person than you please wifey, if the man won't stop his cheating.

I reiterate, WHY, do the 3 or 4 females want to be disturbing a married man that they are not in a Polygamous relationship with.

I ask again, <u>Or are you on Aphrodisiac or Viagra?</u>

It's not very exciting being in a Polygamous relationship with just two women, but 3 or four, that is crazy.

I think 2 females may be certified in a polygamous relationship, but, ABOVE 2 women in a polygamous relationship should be banned.

Without talking too much as I need to hurry up now. I remember when I was in primary school about 9 years old, we played a computer game on the shortest way to do something. The main focus of the game, was, try to be thinking before you do something major, if minor, don't worry then.

I'm going to use my own example as I can't remember the game in the exact format.

For example, I'm not saying you should do this, you can do whatever you like. It's just a small example of if you need to do something on a bigger scale. This might not be a very great example, but it is close.

E.g., getting a glass of juice from the fridge.

Let's say it's only you and your daughter living in your apartment. The table is already set with mugs, or cups or whatever type of cup.

Then you can either:-

- Go to the fridge get the juice and take it to the table, where the juice jug for four serving is; and pour the juice into the juice jug for four serving. Then return the bottle of juice to the fridge.

- Option two, or you could take the juice jug for four serving, to the top of your fridge or to any available table work space, nearby there, pour the juice, put the bottle back into the fridge. Then take the juice jug for four serving, filled with juice to the table.

Last but not the least, how to know if a cup is half full, or half empty.

If a cup is half empty it would be distressed, that's the first indication. If half full, then first indication, is that, no body has touched it yet. SUN 20/02/2022-

(11:17 AM)- Sun 20.FEB/22

Hillsongs: In control; Beneath the waters

Furthermore...

……. (Ps), THERE are probably oral tablets to temporarily stop the flow of a period, when the DR. is carrying out medical examination, I don't know.

FURTHERMORE, Please Note that, anti-psychotics medication taken in broad day light, can be dangerous if abused. If given for a prolonged period of time, it becomes a sedative drug. When it puts you to sleep. The danger of this is,

1. if exposed to the surrounding of the wrong people, you could be abducted,
2. you could be harmed in the sleep, or incapacitated.
3. If there is a fire, you may burn with it.

Again, anti-psychotics medication, can be dangerous if abused. When increased, could prevent the muscles in your hands, from not working properly, may give **tremors,** then instead of being able to fuck yourself through masturbation, **it may lead to sexual captivity in that you may become promiscuous, consequently.**

The flipping psychiatrist, lures you to sleep with a man you are not in love with, to be getting pregnant for him as well. If you refuse to comply, it may lead to further sexual captivity in that you may become promiscuous, consequently, you may catch disease.

Stimulating an individual, to charge him or her <u>up</u> with Viagra, or Aphrodisiac, in order for victim to *level up sexually to those that have become, loose females as well males,* should be punishable. You're going to need deliverance, if you are a Christian O!

Why should other peoples', sexual problems be your problem?

<u>Which I pray it, deliverance,</u> also works, as if the pastor doesn't know/ or if he knows, but doesn't say what is wrong with you...

.......Then you are at the mercy of those giving you a sexual stimulant, after <u>if</u> being sedated with <u>antipsychotic</u> drugs GIVEn IN BROAD DAY LIGHT, that is so called meant to heal your metal health illness O!
<u>Or if the antipsychotic is administered with the intention to harm.</u>

> *KJV Proverbs 9:16-18*

Proverbs 9:16 "Whoso is simple, let turn in hither: and as for him that wanteth understanding, she saith to him,

Proverbs 9:17 "Stolen waters are sweet, and bread eaten in secret is pleasant.

Proverbs 9:18 "But he knoweth not that the dead are there; and that her quests are in the depths of hell." Please note that, some *people are only bloody users, because they don't believe in heaven not to talk of a hell is real. So, they think they can steal other peoples ideas,* DESPITE THE FACT THAT THE victim, is NOT DEAD YET; and get away with God's judgement for their bad behaviour, to cast to hell after death. You don't worry, be rationally giving your things freely, even your money, or fully be giving your things freely, even your money, it's your choice, continue to be good. Though you keep giving your things freely, even your money, but get nothing in return, just abuse plus insults instead.

<u>I used the word bloody, because I want to whom it may concern to have a conscience!</u>

> ## In conclusion

Ifb God gives you either a boy or a girl, treat them both with care. Don't say, it's a boy, he can look after himself when he becomes a man, so don't because of that, abandon him for the father. You need to be part of your child's life, whether it is a boy or a girl. Don't abandon him o.

Also if I were to choose, I'd choose two girls one boy. In an Ideal world, 2 boys, 2 girls.

In addition, never date ▦ a man 🙂, who ask for a large amount of money from you, you like a fool trusted him, when he promises that by one week, the money will be refunded back to you with interest. Because, by the time you might need the money…

……. if he doesn't pay the money back💰, you'll have to go borrow again and then you'll be in debt.

If he cannot accept the 100 pounds max, that you'll offering to borrow him, tell him to piss off or go play with a new twat, because you are not that twat / silly or perhaps, stupid fool anymore~!!!~!!!~6•~

 All you would have lost is a hundred pounds. If after, you borrowed him the money, as you trusted him, but then he betrays your trust; and doesn't pay you back, all you would have lost is a £100.00.

It all depends, if his proposal is genuine, what he wants to borrow the money for, if it's to benefit both of you. However, watch it, if he keeps asking for more and more, it gets to a point when you say, enough is enough. Especially the <u>drawing point and border line</u>, before investing a large amount of money into that relationship, is if he starts to be forceful, trying to get your bank code and all that, you trusted him and gave it to him, then he walks away.

First thing first, change your bank pass code, then move on. This part is sensitive for me to say, but, try not to take him back, especially if you still have feelings for him, be realistic, maybe that relationship weren't meant to be.

Especially, if you yourself, had doubts about if the relationship would work out. <u>Because, it is what it is, you will get over him later...</u>

.... because he was probably not 100% satisfied with you. Or maybe he has a secret lover. Also, man, you need 100% from a man, if a man is not giving his 100%, if not, that relationship might break up along the way.

This is my own suggestions, what do you think on the situation? As, some men and women alike are big pretenders! !!

....

Someone gave me a leaflet or a tract about hell, I think it is interesting, I believe hell is real.

However, somethings classed as sins, I don't actually think anything is wrong with them under given circumstances. I.e. masturbation, listening to secular music, abortion, and divorce, some are OK under given circumstances.

Ps I do believe that Pretence is a sin like mentioned in the tract

Also, this wasn't mentioned, **but,** I don't believe **in** homosexual relationships, lesbians, gay, bisexualism, I think it's wrong, it's not biblical, it's a sin. Though it is something the individual has to come to terms with, it is then their choice. **I'm not judging, I'm just saying.**

Plus if it is allowed to be broadcasted to young people, plus children that, being homosexual gay or lesbian or bisexual, is alright.

Then it should also be allowed to broadcast the Christian values on LGB movement.

First of all noone is judging anyone, but the same right they have to be accepted, is the same right Christian's should have to put their objections across.

Not being allowed, to say nothing about a Christian perspective of LGB movement, is intentionally, making our children's future to be at jeopardy of the truth.

Depriving them of the right path in other words.

It should be a paramount as well vital importance...

.......To be allowed, to project that the Christian values, objects to this kind of behaviour, however, it is a choice that the next generation has to make for themselves.

Not for the church to condemn anyone who wants to be an LGB candidate, not to kick them out of the church, but to keep praying and hoping for them to change their ways, if the young person chooses the LGB path way.

However, that sort of patience may run out, if the individual doesn't change to do the Godly way.

Peace out.

I hope the next selfish from the church they want to take inspiration from, that they treat her better than they did to me. I hope she doesn't get the same I'll treatment plus harassment.

Holier than thou Christians.

Digressing, there's no time for a long explanation, but I feel that the prevention of homelessness is better than the cure.

Also, if you have a little change to spare, try to give to a homeless person, even 50 pence is something.

Once upon a time, in my life I had determined to give every homeless person 2 pounds every day I went out, whenever, I can in contact with one,.

At odd times I was compelled to give 5 or ten pounds. By the end of the month I had given £50 to a couple of homeless people. It all adds up, **but then, I suddenly realised I cannot change their circumstance unless the government helps them.**

The choice is left for the giver to help or not to help with change or not.

I reinforce, that the prevention of homelessness is better than its cure.

First of all, talking about Polygamy. If you are vulnerable, maybe your family should be there to protect you until you grow old. Work with your family, listen to their advice, because they are your guardian Angel, if you rebel, devilish people will deal with you OOO.

But only listen to the family member that you get on with and trust.

Plus, it is one thing to want to listen to your family's instructions it is another for them...

.... to care to want to give you instructions to protect you in the first place. Some family members, …

…….their friends, alliances and associates, put them up to lying to you. Hence, both your family, as well their friends are bloody liars.

A song will follow this statement, that sums up the fact that sometimes we know we ought to be holy, but our flesh, body or soul wants us to sin against God in Fornicating, or to be lured into the wrong relationship though you might not want sex consequently might want to be alone all the days of your life plus then not to have children, ___or if you don't want to have children until Mr right comes along,___ but if you instead you find yourself needing sex, then the question is that who did this to you, because a man caressing a woman or female will turn her on.

This is a natural affection.

But without this natural affection, then may be aphrodisiac is in action like someone is playing games with you, this is forceful affection. Which could lead to, you ending up with a new man or a stranger in your life, either from your country or white a man, a stranger is a stranger at first until you get to know him or her.

However, when all you wanted was to stay single and not have any children. If you don't want marriage, for whatever reason maybe because the point is to have children and enjoy your man. But once again, if because you don't want children, **until Mr right comes along,** then that is your choice.

The devil hides himself as a wolf in sheep's clothing, when someone pretends to be nice but they are not. His mission, is to kill to steal and to destroy. **<u>He is the antagonist</u> _who_** creates animosity within the church, so to divide the church. We as a church are to stand, in solidarity against hatred in the church and the schemes of the d devil.

<u>The other, is legal captivity, which I don't even want to think of examples, as it is negative and for me can be quite disturbing, as well devastating.</u>

Song Title: Holy 'R' you Lord God Almighty?

Holy 7X

Are you Lord God almighty?

Worthy is the Lamb 2X

You are Holy!

Song Title: I want to be Holy unto you

I want to be holy unto to you

I want to be worthy of your name

And as I live this life for you

I declare,

Your majesty and King

Song Title: I behold you

I behold you, Most holy one

I behold you,

As the lamb on the throne

As I worship you

In reverent fear

I behold you

Jesus the Lord.

Let us say for instance a man/woman of God and it should only be a man/woman of God that tells you this, that "God wants you to do polygamy because of the weakness(es) in your life which makes you vulnerable to, possibly subject to abuse, control, manipulation, Or harm, by a secret enemy of yours, or an evil person."

Before you take polygamy, please when they "to whom it may concern," openly shows you your weakness which is the reason why they said God said you need to do Polygamy marriage in the first place; and you must get this proof, but why does there have to be a weakness, why don't God just tell you what job he wants you to do without any buts in your life.

When you are satisfied with the decision, but I would advise you can use pills if you want to, but don't use the contraceptives, such as IUS SHORT FOR INTRAUTERINE SYSTEM IN THE MEDICAL TERM coils, nor get a vasectomy/ Sterilisations. But condoms are good, though some people don't like condom, for whatever reason best known to them, then you will have to find a natural method of contraceptive then if you don't like condoms, **as condoms can split at the side, also it could, but not saying definitely, but if the man is going too fast, it could go up you and you might need to go hospital to get it out. However,** but if you have one child already, then have no more than three more or less than < three more.

Note IUS SHORT FOR INTRAUTERINE SYSTEM 36 IN THE MEDICAL TERM, coils, may or may not cause ectopic pregnancy, also, when you distress your womb with different medical procedures may or may not cause ectopic pregnancy. Avoid using contraceptives during your period/menstruation, unless advice by a professional gynaecologists.

Also, there may be spotting of blood at the start of using some contraceptives. **Also,** I reiterate Condoms, on the other hand are ok, but be careful, because, if your man goes too fast, it could go up deep into you, also, condom/rubber, could split at the side, so be careful o.

Some men are evil they are there to teach you a stupid message as you'd get the point faster if you get dumped or you had to dump them after a year of no marriage plus when not fornicating with them, why do they have to be so nasty, don't let them touch you, it would have been better if they married you, but they play games with you, then leave you broken and go off with the next selfish.

Furthermore, When sperm is released into a woman if you see your period after, then this means your womb is infertile as the sperm did not form. The period cleanses out your system. But don't give up God can still make the infertile womb fertile.

Also, I don't know why a singlet woman or female needs sex, if she doesn't have her own man to herself. Sex is for intimacy between two people who love each other; and their children are birth out of Love. Not to be having sex with silly men that you are not in love with.

Those females, who are sleeping with a married man obliviously, that is the man lies that he is single, when he is not single but is married, the female sleeping temporarily with a married man till you get your own, or sleeping with a man who has a girlfriend. This is wrong, because there is nothing God cannot stop. If you pray hard enough, God will remove the urge to have sex outside wedlock, esp' with a married man.

As soon as you find out that he is married or that he has a girlfriend, but make sure that his girlfriend or wife is alright with it. You don't have to stop it immediately, but you will have to pray your way out of the situation ASAP because you really need to be holy like God is, if you don't have your own man.

Also, I reiterate, reinforce and repeat, men if you are an engineer, face your work and love your wife, stop chasing a single woman to see what's going on in her life, don't go hurting a single person, don't be selfish you have your own wife. If the single woman accepts you then let that be her choice, don't lure or coheres her into a relationship with you, when you have a wife, are you trying to enslave her or something?

Make sure that you try not to do polygamy but try to focus on whatever job you do i.e., engineer, pharmacist, DR, lawyer, house wife, ministry work, child minder/ Nanny; and don't get confused in doing polygamy with whoever, as we'll get the point a lot faster by now.

If you're unemployed, Know that you are not a lone, there are others in that situations as you, keep praying, keep knocking on those doors; and I believe, God will open a door for you. You will get a good job one day, if you don't give up.

Any relationship, whether monogamous, or Polygamous, we need to prayerfully choose these partners, as either could end up in heart break. On the other hand, Polygamy is your choice and can be done in exceptional cases, if the two women get along, but I don't like it.

I just feel that if you can't get any men in these categories, then what's the point, again it's your choice. Why not be holy even as God is holy then?

This brings me to the point that you need to be careful not to go with a man who is divorced or a woman who has for the wrong reasons divorced their partner, like if the man or woman is a cheat, he or she might cheat on you too.

But **Some** divorced people are ok, so make sure you ask questions and get to know him or her well before saying yes to him or her.

Because some people like I was, would never compromise their standards as a Christian, Fornication would be a sin, so therefore, wouldn't have it any other way than to get married before having sex.

 The man then marries her, even though he had another woman he was going to marry before her. Then when, she finds out about his mistress, she refuses to do Polygamy.

So, some people they divorced because instead of a broken courtship, they rush into marriage and then do it that way instead. Hence that relationship was whatever. **_Besides, if no one knows why you kept getting your first sexual urge,_** then like the bible says in KJV 1 Corinthians 7:8-9 if a man burns he should marry.

1 Cor 7:8 "I say therefore to the unmarried and widows, It is good for them even if they abide even as I."

1 Cor 7:9 "But if they cannot contain, let them marry: for it is better to marry than to burn."

But Fornication due to Viagra is not your fault but it just shows that the devil and that man or woman, took advantage of you at your weakest point, however way you want to look at it, fight the good fight of faith and don't sleep around.

Before every sexual partner, please let him and you get tested if he won't do it, dump him. You may date men in these categories: -

- ❖ A divorced man who has had girlfriends after marriage, but has to be single and is actually divorced for the right reason; and is definitely single ¾
- ❖ A younger person than you who is actually single
- ❖ — A man whose wife is deceased or late and died and is actually single

In all of these cases you have to pray and have peace in your heart that you trust the younger guy or older man; and any older single man you meet.

But concerning the nanny/childminder who gets on with her job, cannot a man of God or woman of God, a clergy or priest, monitor her so that she behaves herself, so that she doesn't do anything bad to other people's children. Good luck and God bless.

I just feel that some problems in life will never end until Christ comes back again to heal the world of its hurts and pains, so when life throws problems at you, hold on to your faith with full force and pray.

However, Polygamy without the consent of the singlet lady, should be against the law plus illegal, meaning irrespective of her vulnerability or the silly lesson about life; and her naivety, the man wants to teach her, if a married man doesn't tell a singlet single lady the truth about his marital status in due time preferably immediately, as a married man should get the consent of the single woman, about if she wants to continue with the married man. *If a man is caught lying to a* singlet *lady, about* his marital status, *he should be prosecuted by giving him a lenient fine, if not prosecuted by man, will be persecuted by the Angel of God.*

Digressing. Like any type of Rape, any type of Trespassing is a criminal offence, I need not remind you!!!

Though I don't know, what female will want to go on with this. 72 Nevertheless, it's a matter of personal choice. Whether it is legal for a man to be allowed to have a girlfriend and a wife, or whether a man is allowed to legally have two wives.

The point is, when a married man wants to teach a vulnerable woman a lesson about life; and her naivety, then it is at the discretion of the Police, the church clergy and that man; and especially, He has a responsibility to tell the single lady, his girlfriend the truth about his marital status in due time. Once more, I reiterate and I reinforce, it is at the discretion of the Police, the church clergy; and at the discretion of the Police, the church clergy and that man but I do not know why they have to lie.

But I reiterate, if a man would truly love a woman/female, why don't the man of God send the right man to you in the first place, why do they always have to prove a point, **when the wrong man comes to you to deceive.**

He has a responsibility to tell the single lady, his girlfriend the truth about his marital status in due time ***preferably, immediately.***

At the end of the day, it all comes down to the fact that the truth has to be told at the right time. Also, if it is the case that, should polygamy be legalised? Because if a man wants to marry to wives, that is what he should say. A man being allowed to permanently deceive a woman means then, that the government is slack in their duty to protect vulnerable adults from conduits.

Polygamy is only wrong and is only an abuse for a woman, if it's against the consent of my God of Jesus Christ; and the male in question, has to get the consent of the female in question as well.

Otherwise, What do you need sex for, if you are a singlet? Maybe you should wait your turn. Polygamy should be done with someone that you know well a close relative not a close family friend whom you don't like the look of them, like she cannot be trusted, or is perhaps a control freak, hence dodgy.

<u>But only God knows why he wants you to share your man. However, I'm not knocking Polygamy, prayerfully consider polygamy with a close relative or in other words, a close family member, I repeat, not a close family friend or stranger, whom you don't like the look of them, like she cannot be trusted, or is perhaps a control freak, hence dodgy.</u>

5 reasons when Polygamy is wrong!

1. Lying about the man's wife with intentions to lure into Polygamy or girlfriend to be in a polyamory relationship. This is not good because if the woman knew the truth in the first place, she might decide that actually, she don't want to get involved in Polygamy.
2. When a woman is forced into Polygamy.
3. When a man marries a woman and tells her after marriage to her that she is the second wife.
4. When the man marries a woman and has side chicks, this opens doors to sexually transmitted diseases. This is wrong wrong wrong. Maybe she don't want to do Polygamy, as this to me is counted as another form of polygamy, sharing your man with whoever; and you aren't informed about it, this should be illegal, and legally banned if caught reprimanded etc.
5. If a man threatens a woman into doing Polygamy. All these reasons are the 5 reasons when Polygamy is wrong!

<u>King James Version</u> (KJV) 1 Samuel *26 : 8-12*

8 "Then said Abishai to David, God hath delivered thine enemy into thine hand this day: now therefore let me smite him, I pray thee, with the spear even to the earth at once, and I will not smite him the second time."

9 "And David said to Abishai, Destroy him not: for who can stretch forth his hand against the LORD's anointed, and be guiltless?"

10 "David said furthermore, As the LORD liveth, the LORD shall smite him; or his day shall come to die; or he shall descend into battle, and perish."

11 "The LORD forbid that I should stretch forth mine hand against the LORD's anointed: but, I pray thee, take thou now the spear that is at his bolster, and the cruse of water, and let us go."

12 "<u>So David took the spear and the cruse</u> *of water from Saul's bolster;* and they gat them away, and no man saw it, nor knew it, neither awaked: for they were *all asleep; because a deep sleep from the LORD was fallen* upon them."

<u>New international version</u> (NIV) 1 Samuel 26 : 8-12

8 "Abishai said to David, "Today God has delivered your enemy into your hands. Now let me pin him to the ground with one thrust of the spear; I won't strike him twice."

9 "But David said to Abishai, "Don't destroy him! Who can lay a hand on the LORD's anointed and be guiltless?"

10 "As surely as the LORD lives," he said, "the LORD himself will strike him, or his time will come and he will die, or he will go into battle and perish."

11 "But the LORD forbid that I should lay a hand on the LORD's anointed. Now get the spear and water jug that are near his head, and let's go."

12 "So David took the spear and water jug near Saul's head, and they left. No one saw or knew about it, nor did anyone wake up. They were all sleeping, because the LORD had put them into a deep sleep."

. . . .

1 Samuel 26 : 8-9.........*This shows that vulnerable people are at the mercy of those around them.*

Where there is love you will last, even if you are vulnerable. Meaning if you have a good man by your side, you will be just fine.

8 "Abishai said to David, "Today God has delivered your enemy into your hands. Now let me pin him to the ground with one thrust of the spear; I won't strike him twice."

9 "But David said to Abishai, "Don't destroy him! Who can lay a hand on the LORD's anointed and be guiltless?"

KJV I Samuel 28:1-20

I Samuel 28: 1 "And it came to pass in those days, that the Philistines gathered their armies together for warfare, to fight with Israel. And Achish said unto David, Know thou assuredly, that thou shalt go out with me to battle, thou and thy men."

I Samuel 28:2 "And David said to Achish, Surely thou shalt know what thy servant can do. And Achish said to David, Therefore will I make thee keeper of mine head for ever."

I Samuel 28:3 Now Samuel was dead, and all Israel had lamented him, and buried him in Ramah, even in his own city. And Saul had put away those that had familiar spirits, and the wizards, out of the land.

I Samuel 28: 4 And the Philistines gathered themselves together, and came and pitched in Shunem: and Saul gathered all Israel together, and they pitched in Gilboa.

I Samuel 28: 5 And when Saul saw the host of the Philistines, he was afraid, and his heart greatly trembled.

I Samuel 28: 6 And when Saul enquired of the Lord, the Lord answered him not, neither by dreams, nor by Urim, nor by prophets.

I Samuel 28: 7 Then said Saul unto his servants, Seek me a woman that hath a familiar spirit, that I may go to her, and enquire of her. And his servants said to him, Behold, there is a woman that hath a familiar spirit at Endor.

I Samuel 28: 8 And Saul disguised himself, and put on other raiment, and he went, and two men with him, and they came to the woman by night: and he said, I pray thee, divine unto me by the familiar spirit, and bring me him up, whom I shall name unto thee.

I Samuel 28: 11 Then said the woman, Whom shall I bring up unto thee? And he said, Bring me up Samuel.

I Samuel 28: 12 And when the woman saw Samuel, she cried with a loud voice: and the woman spake to Saul, saying, Why hast thou deceived me? for thou art Saul.

I Samuel 28: 13 And the king said unto her, Be not afraid: for what sawest thou? And the woman said unto Saul, I saw gods ascending out of the earth.

I Samuel 28: 14 And he said unto her, What form is he of? And she said, An old man cometh up; and he is covered with a mantle. And Saul perceived that it was Samuel, and he stooped with his face to the ground, and bowed himself.

I Samuel 28: 15 And Samuel said to Saul, Why hast thou disquieted me, to bring me up? And Saul answered, I am sore distressed; for the Philistines make war against me, and God is departed from me, and answereth me no more, neither by prophets, nor by dreams: therefore I have called thee, that thou mayest make known unto me what I shall do.

I Samuel 28: 16 Then said Samuel, Wherefore then dost thou ask of me, seeing the Lord is departed from thee, and is become thine enemy?

I Samuel 28: 17 And the Lord hath done to him, as he spake by me: for the Lord hath rent the kingdom out of thine hand, and given it to thy neighbour, even to David:

I Samuel 28: 18 Because thou obeyedst not the voice of the Lord, nor executedst his fierce wrath upon Amalek, therefore hath the Lord done this thing unto thee this day.

I Samuel 28:19 Moreover the Lord will also deliver Israel with thee into the hand of the Philistines: and to morrow shalt thou and thy sons be with me: the Lord also shall deliver the host of Israel into the hand of the Philistines.

I Samuel 28:20 "Then Saul fell straightway all along on the earth, and was sore afraid, because of the words of Samuel: and there was no strength in him; for he had eaten no bread all the day, nor all the night."

KJV I Sam 31:1-6

I Sam 31:1 "Now the Philistines fought against Israel: and the men of Israel fled from before the Philistines, and fell down slain in mount Gilboa.

I Sam 31:2 And the Philistines followed hard upon Saul and upon his sons; and the Philistines slew Jonathan, and Abinadab, and Melchishua, Saul's sons.

I Sam 31:3 And the battle went sore against Saul, and the archers hit him; and he was sore wounded of the archers.

I Sam 31:4 Then said Saul unto his armourbearer, Draw thy sword, and thrust me through therewith; lest these uncircumcised come and thrust me through, and abuse me. But his armourbearer would not; for he was sore afraid. Therefore Saul took a sword, and fell upon it.

I Sam 31:5 And when his armourbearer saw that Saul was dead, he fell likewise upon his sword, and died with him.

I Sam 31:6 So Saul died, and his three sons, and his armourbearer, and all his men, that same day together."

I Sam 31:3-4 Saul went to a witch to prophecy about his future, as God had departed from him. The bible records it as that, Saul went to a woman that has a familiar spirit. Who brought up the spirit of a dead prophet, Samuel, it was this spirit

of the dead prophet Samuel's that prophecies to him, what would be Saul's, later doom.

He found out that he was doomed for destruction. This can't have been an easy news for him to carry but he walked in his fate. Saul's enemy the philistines slew him and he had to finish it off by killing himself as they only wounded him but not killed him, in order to avoid, further abuse from the enemy.

Digressing, also know that not everyone that goes to church is a Christian. I also suspect that your natural controllable sexual urge can be topped to an unusual level, when each time you feel like having sex, both white and black men that aren't your type, could approach you. What is all this about I don't know. Not because they are ugly, but they are just not your type. Or some could not be your type because, not very physically attractive either.

Because I don't think that a woman should be going into a relationship just because of sexual urges, but because she actually loves the man. Note, when she wanted to have a baby with a guy she loved, her womb was infertile due to the side effects of her antipsychotic drug. But now they want her to get pregnant for other men that she doesn't love because of Viagra. So, I have come to warn you the reader of this book, to be careful.

This is a very wicked and obscene behaviour, it is criminal and an injustice under the sun, note also that, if care is not taken, <u>some children when born, could</u> be brought into the world to be made <u>subject of medical experiments.</u> I'm not <u>saying this is always the case, but if care is not taken.</u> Children are to be born in a loving relationship where two people love and care about each other. Children are not toys, to be made as a means of medical examinations.

What kind of God makes someone have gifts and then makes them vulnerable so that others can be enjoying their gift after when they kill the vulnerable person. You might as well be the nanny or housemaid that they wanted you to be in the first place. I smell something fishy. Something fishy is going on. Because God is good all the time, he has a reason for every one of his creations.

✠ THE TEN COMMANDMENTS

KJV - King James Version

Exodus 20:1-26

Exodus 20:1 And God spake all these words, saying,

Exodus 20:2 I am the Lord thy God, which have brought thee out of the land of Egypt, out of the house of bondage.

1. Exodus 20:3 Thou shalt have no other gods before me.
2. Exodus 20:4 Thou shalt not make unto thee any graven image, or any likeness of any thing that is in heaven above, or that is in the earth beneath, or that is in the water under the earth.

Continuation of commandment 2. Exodus 20:5 Thou shalt not bow down thyself to them, nor serve them: for I the Lord thy God am a jealous God, visiting the iniquity of the fathers upon the children unto the third and fourth generation of them that hate me;

Exodus 20:6 And shewing mercy unto thousands of them that love me, and keep my commandments.

3. Exodus 20:7 Thou shalt not take the name of the Lord thy God in vain; for the Lord will not hold him guiltless that taketh his name in vain.
4. Exodus 20:8 Remember the sabbath day, to keep it holy.
5. Exodus 20:9 Six days shalt thou labour, and do all thy work:

Exodus 20:10 But the seventh day is the sabbath of the Lord thy God: in it thou shalt not do any work, thou, nor thy son, nor thy daughter, thy manservant, nor thy maidservant, nor thy cattle, nor thy stranger that is within thy gates:

Exodus 20:11 For in six days the Lord made heaven and earth, the sea, and all that in them is, and rested the seventh day: wherefore the Lord blessed the sabbath day, and hallowed it.

6. Exodus 20:12 Honour thy father and thy mother: that thy days may be long upon the land which the Lord thy God giveth thee.
7. Exodus 20:13 Thou shalt not kill.
8. Exodus 20:14 Thou shalt not commit adultery.
9. Exodus 20:15 Thou shalt not steal.
10. Exodus 20:16 Thou shalt not bear false witness against thy neighbour.

Exodus 20:17 Thou shalt not covet thy neighbour's house, thou shalt not covet thy neighbour's wife, nor his manservant, nor his maidservant, nor his ox, nor his ass, nor any thing that is thy neighbour's.

Exodus 20:18 And all the people saw the thunderings, and the lightnings, and the noise of the trumpet, and the mountain smoking: and when the people saw it, they removed, and stood afar off.

Exodus 20:19 And they said unto Moses, Speak thou with us, and we will hear: but let not God

speak with us, lest we die.

Exodus 20:20 And Moses said unto the people, Fear not: for God is come to prove you, and that his fear may be before your faces, that ye sin not.

Exodus 20:21 And the people stood afar off, and

Moses drew near unto the thick darkness where God was.

Exodus 20:22 And the Lord said unto Moses, Thus thou shalt say unto the children of Israel, Ye have seen that I have talked with you from heaven.

Exodus 20:23 Ye shall not make with me gods of silver, neither shall ye make unto you gods of gold.

Exodus 20:24 An altar of earth thou shalt make unto me, and shalt sacrifice thereon thy burnt offerings, and thy peace offerings, thy sheep, and thine oxen: in all places where I record my name I will come unto thee, and

I will bless thee.

Exodus 20:25 And if thou wilt make me an altar of stone, thou shalt not build it of hewn stone: for if thou lift up thy tool upon it, thou hast polluted it.

Exodus 20:26 Neither shalt thou go up by steps unto mine altar, that thy nakedness be not discovered thereon.

Focusing on "Thou shalt not kill," This is to say, do not take away your life or other people's lives. Hell is real, whether hell on earth first from strange people with strange powers, or from the Tyrant, an oppressive ruler, women with the spirit of Jezebel etc. etc.

Then the real hell which the bible describes in King James Version

Revelations 21:8 "But the fearful, and unbelieving, and the abominable, and murderers, and whoremongers, and sorcerers, and idolaters, and all liars, shall have their part in the lake which burneth with fire and brimstone: which is the second death."

God is loving; and only he knows who he will let into heaven, even after if you commit suicide for a silly reason.

Is it that you need more patience, why do you want to commit suicide, or just as bad, why do you want to kill another brother or sister? When, you didn't create them-!!!- !!!-6-

Mat 5:22 "But I say unto you, That whosoever is angry with his brother without a cause shall be in danger of the judgment: and whosoever shall say to his brother, Raca, shall be in danger of the council: but whosoever shall say, Thou fool, shall be in danger of hell fire."

If you have no real reason to commit suicide don't. Especially, don't be an hater for no apparent reason, God is watching you.

2. Exodus 20:4 Thou shalt not make unto thee any graven image, or any likeness of any thing that is in heaven above, or that is in the earth beneath, or that is in the water under the earth.

Continuation of commandment 2. Exodus 20:5 Thou shalt not bow down thyself to them, nor serve them: for I the Lord thy God am a jealous God, visiting the iniquity of the fathers upon the children unto the third and fourth generation of them that hate me;

What eXODUS 20:4-5 is simply saying is that, don't create graven images for the sake to turn them into worship idols, in replacement of worshiping and serving God. It's not creating the graven images that is the problem, it is the worship of them.

If not, all those graven images of important men, warriors of British myths and past British heroines, the big lion in Trafalgar square, plus the statue of liberty in New York, are all wrong then.

Mat 22: 35 "Then one of them, which was a lawyer, asked him a question, tempting him, and saying,"

36 "Master, which is the great commandment in the law?"

37 "Jesus said unto him, Thou shalt love the Lord thy God with all thy heart, and with all thy soul, and with all thy mind."

38 "This is the first and great commandment."

39 "And the second is like unto it, Thou shalt love thy neighbour as thyself."

I Joh 4:12 "No man hath seen God at any time. If we love one another, God dwelleth in us, and his love is perfected in us."

I Joh 3:15 "Whosoever hateth his brother is a murderer: and ye know that no murderer hath eternal life abiding in him."

I want to tell you a story about a lady, who was afraid to sleep at night.

As, once, she found herself in an awkward position in bed. She found herself in a situation, whereby, when she woke up, she was laying at an angle, with adjacent to the shortest width of the double size bed.

Basically, she was scared that someone was coming through the wall, like witches with strange powers, were coming through the walls, at night to touch her.

As she locks her door, with security measure, e.g., she has a gate at the outer court, by which she only has the key to. Unless of course the council has spare keys and didn't inform her about it on purpose.

So, plus, there is no way they could have come through the door without the council secretly having spare keys. God bless... ....byeeeee.

Even if you were to see a ghost, God forbid, the mental health people would still try to say you were not well, instead of investigating, they are quick to judge and throw people into psychiatric wards.

Anyway she got takento psychiatric hospital for hallucination and then her medication was increased.

This is what I have to say about this,...

.... first of all, all that about someone is coming through the wall to get her was the wrong attitude to have.

Though, I sympathise with her, such magic do not exist. The worst that could happen is that, if at all you left your shoes in front of the door as you came in, the night or day before, whatever hr of the day before. Then if the council has the spare keys of your outer court gate. Maybe they let a magician plus witch DR, come in at night to have repositioned you on the bed. That is not nice, it's wicked I'm telling you this now.

The job of the magician, like as seen on TV, would be to reposition your shoes back to the position you put it the night before, as seen this type of magic on TV. Please, note, this is not hYPNOSIS.

Even if such magic, witchcraft, sorcery, does exist, which I am strongly doubting, you don't go telling psychiatrist about that, they'll just think you are not well.

What you do is you keep locking your door with safety measures, install alarms with a passcode, if you must or something.

Because even if you were to see a ghost, God forbid, the mental health people would still try to say you were not well, instead of investigating, they are quick to judge and throw people into psychiatric wards.

 Because I believe, there is a God in heaven, who is watching over you and I, if we are in line in the faith of Jesus Christ.So then plead the blood of Jesus, anytime you want to, over your life and your home. Then, that demon, or devil worshiper, or evil angel instead of a good angel, or magician will have to bow to the name of Jesus and stop harassing you in your home.

Matthew 25:41
King James Version

41 "Then shall he say also unto them on the left hand, Depart from me, ye cursed, into everlasting fire, prepared for the devil and his angels:"

You take the authority over your life: and declare the name of Jesus, the devil has got to give up over your life. So please never you imagine such again, that someone like a magician is coming through the walls, even if they are, I cannot stress more than this, the Nme of Jesus is your weapon of warfare against the enemy and the evil one.

tHIS WILL REMAIN A MYSTERY.

Peace be with you.

Philippians 4:7
King James Version

7 "And the peace of God, which passeth all understanding, shall keep your hearts and minds through Christ Jesus."

Also, note I reinforce that, no one can open your door, unless if it's an unscrupulous dishonest, dodgy, individual or friend, you gave spare keys to your flat to. Or if it's an unscrupulous landlord, who is actually allowed spare keys to your flat in the first place, legally.

Then if the council has the spare keys of your outer court gate. They let a magician plus witch DR, come in at night to have repositioned you on the bed. That is not nice, it's wicked I'm telling you this now.

The job of the magician, like as seen on TV, would be to reposition your shoes back to the position you put it the night before, as seen this type of magic on TV. Please, note, this is not hYPNOSIS.

tHIS WILL REMAIN A MYSTERY.

As seen on TV b4. Before, I've seen how a magician, scattered some items from how it was laid or set out. Then used magical powers, to reset or rearranged the items back to it's original composition or layout.

Philippians 4:7
King James Version

7 "And the peace of God, which passeth all understanding, shall keep your hearts and minds through Christ Jesus."

Let everyone testify, that God is good and his mercies endures forever; and that Jesus Christ is Lord.

If you are single, you'll live a different life, from when married. Things you did when you were single will change.

I.e., When you are now married,

1. at any time of the day be it morning, afternoon or evening, when tiding up. Try not to obstruct the main entrance door way, by leaving a bucket of mop water, there.
2. <u>*or by leaving*</u> your shoes in front of the door as you came in, the night or day before, whatever hr of the day before, ***When you are now married, remember you are not alone now, your man is now there, plus your man is there to protect you O!-!!!-***

More so, in the first case:-

- **If your family member comes to open the door at the wrong time, the water in the mop bucket will spill all over the carpet or vinyl. You'll have to clean it up again, you could even slip if it is vinyl.**

Second case:-

- *If your family member comes to open the door at the wrong time, when* your shoes were left in front of the door as you came in, the night or day before, whatever hr of the day before, The door will shift it out of the way anyways so try not to obstruct the door way.

- **God bless.**

First of all we need to acknowledge that we are sinners and that we need to give our lives to Christ then to be saved from going to hell after this life. John 3:16 [for God so loved the world that he gave his only begotten son, that whosoever believes in him should not perish, but have everlasting life].

When we confess that we are sinners and accept the salvation of Christ, God gives us the holy spirit the spirit of truth to help us.

John 3:6-8 kjv "That which is born of the f lesh is f lesh; and that which is born of the spirit is spirit."

7 "Marvel not that I said unto thee, Ye must be born again."

8 "The wind bloweth where it listeth; and thou hearest the sound thereof, but cannot tell whence it cometh, and whither it goeth: so is everyone that is born of the spirit."

This means we need to be born again to be the followers of Christ. Jesus also said in John 14:6 [I am the way, the truth and the life, no man cometh to the father except by me." So give your life to Christ.

You need to be baptised by immersion in water. Mat 3 :13 KJV "Then cometh Jesus from Galilee to Jordan unto John., to be baptised of him."

In Mark 16 :15 KJV "And he said unto them, Go ye into all the world, and preach the gospel to every creature."

16 : he that believeth and is baptized shall be saved; but he that believeth not shall be damned."

Be sober be vigilant and do not be ignorant of the devises of the devil he is a rip off a cunt just like his followers. All these people want to do is _harm_ people so that you can be feeling fat on their drugs, so you can watch them enjoy life whilst you are miserable.

And believe you me, the word miserable is not in the dictionary for no reason you know.

Shall the wicked prosper, I hope they wont.

<u>Your knowledge of your condition will determine give you a better informed decision. Joh 8 :32</u>

32 "And ye shall know the truth, and the truth shall make you free."

It is like being incarcerated and in conf inement when you are under the mental health support. They abuse their office stimulating you sexually so that you can sleep with a man you are not interested in then when you start to get angry they give you high dosage of antipsychotics to shut you up.

You're like a puppet, whilst other bitches are enjoying a good fuck, driving cars and living their dreams, you are being wasted, when imprisoned by psychiatric drugs. This is insane.

They think you have mental illness, but wait till after a baby then they block your womb thereafter, for your one child to come and know what hell on earth is all about.

These antipsychotic drugs are controlling, everything what God said you shouldn't do, when you are taking them, they make you to disobey the will of God.

Fasting becomes difficult, you eat and get fat instead, your sex drive comes on and you start to have sex outside wedlock, fornication.

I think after your depression, the drugs are supposed to be stopped, but instead the psychiatrist keep forcing you to stay on it like you are some sort of criminal, who is in prison.

They could just pick on you; randomly section you if you are noncompliant. Who the hell are all these people? If they got something to say about taking you out of this world then they should be a man about it and come to the open about it. They are dishonest people, in Uniform; and I have no respect for people who molest people e and eventually kills them with their drugs in broad day light without their knowledge...

.... Yes, I will die one day, but not like this, not through lies and manipulations. <u>I'm not saying the authorities</u>

will kill you definitely, but just to be aware of the possibility of manipulation. *Sex, lies and your Soul.*

Tell me why anyone would want to bring children into the world, to come and know all about hell on earth. Then as the children grow up to be ADULTs, to be watching their pairs have a good sex with their partners and good life, whilst they suffer in silence, o go get lost then.

In broad day light, there is so much pressure to get slept with by different men and excuse me for being explicit, ***<u>there are some things you might miss whilst in a relationship, plus you might get used to the sex as well.</u>***

Because, some people, they are palaba.

<u>**So basically,**</u> they wet your appetite, but then every time you are messed about by different men.

Also, a woman who has vagina hair (this *is a clear indication that she is vulnerable).*

<u>*But I still believe that, where there is love you will last, even if you are vulnerable. Meaning if you have a good man by your side, you* will be just fine.</u>

If it were that you only have, armpit hair we'd get the point a lot faster that you are *vulnerable*. If they don't want you to be with the man of your dreams plus they don't want you to enjoy sex with the man you love, then, why are they giving you Viagra for.

I reinforce two ways sex drive can be turned on stimulated. When two people who are attracted to each other touch. Or by the influence of a sex drug, potion Or stimulant, aphrodisiac/Viagra.

IDIOTS.

But as a child of God, you have to be strong and get yourself together.

Don't let your body dictate your sex drive, take charge today. With prayer and a strong will, focus, you can overcome the temptations of the f lesh. Say no, to lack of control of a sexual urge, until you meet the right person.

Also, I know this is a _old fashion way of thinking_, _try_ not to fornicate, _try_ to get married before having sex.

Be careful of forces of darkness witchcraft powers

Witchcraft powers are real, there are people out there who can use voodoo to give you bad luck. So be careful.

- *If witchcraft was not real,* then why can a sexual stimulant work instead of natural sexual urges that comes when a person loves someone and is touched by the person he or she loves.
- *If witchcraft was not real, why are some women made to have male features, hair in odd places, pop belly, long feet for a average height person like Pinocchio.*
- *and many more flaws and blemishes.*
- **If witchcraft was not real, Why do people get bad luck in their lives.**
- **Things that could be inconvenient or even worse case scenario, that are bad exist, such as, why are some women made to have male features, hair in odd places, or even pop belly, long feet for a average height person like Pinocchio and many more flaws and blemishes.**
- **Similarly bad things like, why do people have cancer, bowel cancer, cervical cancer, cancer of any sort, miscarriages as well bad luck.**
- **Why do people get sexually transmitted disease, transgender and terminal illness.**

Though examples of the above may not be the cause of witchcraft, but are stemmed from evil people who either medically neglect you, or manipulate you. And manipulation is like unto witchcraft. For example, giving you drugs that makes your stomach expand more than necessary, or giving a child the medication to make his or her feet longer than his/her height, are all evil.

If care is not taken as a female and adult, men will just use you and dump you, I pray you don't go sleeping around, and catch something, maybe you should be holy like God is *until you get a mister right then.* Sex Lies and your soul.

Names associated with witchcraft

- *The Nigerian's call it Juju*
- *The English call it : Witch craft or Voodoo*
- *The Caribbean's call it : Obeah*

KJV Luke 21:7 And they asked him, saying, Master, but when shall these things be ? and what sign will there be when these things shall come to pass?

Luke 21: 8 And he said, Take heed that ye be not deceived: for many shall come in my name, saying, I am Christ; and the time draweth near: go ye not therefore after them.

<u>Luke 21:9 But when ye shall hear of wars and commotions, be not terrified: for these things must first come to pass ; but the end is not by and by.</u>

<u>Luke 21:10 Then said he unto them, Nation shall rise against nation, and kingdom against kingdom :</u>

Luke 21:11 And great earthquakes shall be in divers places, and famines, and pestilences; and fearful sights and great signs shall there be from heaven.

<u>Luke 21:12 But before all these, they shall lay their hands on you, and persecute you, delivering you up to the synagogues, and into prisons, being brought before kings and rulers for my name's sake.</u>

Luke 21:13 And it shall turn to you for a testimony.

Luke 21:14 Settle it therefore in your hearts, not to meditate before what ye shall answer:

Luke 21:15 For I will give you a mouth and wisdom, which all your adversaries shall not be able to gainsay nor resist.

Luke 21:16 And ye shall be betrayed both by parents, and brethren, and kinsfolks, and friends; and some of you shall they cause to be put to death.

Luke 21:17 And ye shall be hated of all men for my name's sake.

Luke 21:18 But there shall not an hair of your head perish. <u>Luke 21:19 In your patience possess ye your souls.</u>

Be careful of traitors, as we live in an age whereby selfish, cheatalicious people and bloody users are about. So be on your guard.

Be careful not to get into trouble with the police, because you will get locked up. Based on my experience, going to a psychiatric ward or using their drugs, is the same thing as being bound in a prison cell. Your life is going nowhere.

For example, when you go to work, if you get bullied and you report it, they do nothing, instead, you end up under the inf luence of psychiatric drugs for depression and stress related conditions. You can't work, you can't drive, because of the side effects of the drugs. A prolong prescription of it,…

I think becomes unnecessary, it is to make you better, when you are sick i.e., (stressed, depressed, etcetera etc.). Sorry not trying to be funny just saying frankly what anti-psychotics are for.

Sometimes you are not even taught properly the highway code to driving and to pass your theory and practical driving test, HEAVEN KNOWS why!

This is why you need to keep a watch on driving principles, watch it before you lose it.

O I don't know, whatever.

✠ I just want to add that here in <u>West Yorkshire,</u> Sat 19.05.2018, during the Royal wedding, I went to learn how to ride a bicycle, though I had plans to keep up with the wedding at some point during the day and I did. Anyhow, I learnt how to ride a bicycle, it was a fascinating experience, though out of all of the training, I can recall that, in order not to strain your leg, you need to adjust the seat, in such a way that your feet are pointing to the floor, about barely touching the floor. So that after scooting with your comfortable leg which mine is my right leg, I'm right-handed, after scooting with my right leg to then lift of to launch with my right leg, I would not strain that leg when trying to find the pedal to launch on that right pedal.

✠ Overall cycling is Great, most especially great for riding in the park with the children, *<u>but driving a car is better, since the road is predominantly for vehicles not bicycles.</u>* Take care and God bless, but don't cycle on the road if you don't have the confidence to cycle on the road. However, cycle on the pavement or road wherever you're most comfortable.

✠ If you neither want to drive nor learn how to ride a bicycle, that's fine. So then, if a disabled person can drive, so then, if I had to pick 1, I'd rather not ride a bicycle, but I'd rather learn how to drive, than ride a bicycle on the main road. So be careful, I won't say more than that. I don't mind cycling maybe in the park or something.

✠ *If you find a man of God that will prophecy to you, then that is good. So then, if the man of God prophecies anything to you from don't go out with a man, you can ignore him and be careful with that man and study him, then any bad sign from the man you may dump him quickly, then that will be the prophecy of the man of God coming true. But do not go riding on the main road, or on the pavement, especially not on the main road <u>as you don't need it,</u> I would believe his prophecy, that something bad* *might happen regarding this type of prophecy. I would go learn how to drive a car instead.*

✠ Lastly, if someone tells you something won't take long and it ends up taking longer to get to your destination. Do not threat nor fear. Just hold on; as well, don't let that not to give someone your trust again. Next time, double check with that individual, i.e with the relevant, train station Assistant, in order to be sure of what you heard.

✠ *Do not take awkward food on the bus to eat it i.e. Mcflurry ice cream if you don't have a place to put it after you've eaten it or not finished eating it, you could hurt yourself whilst getting off the bus if you cannot get a grip.*

✠ Other names God is known by!
✠ *Jehovah Nisi - his banner over us is Love*
✠ *Jehovah Shammah - our God is ever present*
✠ *Jehovah Jireh - God my provider can also be found somewhere in the book of Genesis*
✠ *Jehovah Sidkenu - God our righteousness*
✠ *Jehovah Rapha - God my healer*
✠ Alpha and omega

✠ <u>Malachi 3:8-10</u>
✠ <u>King James Version</u>

✠ Mal 3:8 *Will a man rob God? Yet ye have robbed me. But ye say, Wherein have we robbed thee? In tithes and offerings.*

✠ Mal 3:8 9 *Ye are cursed with a curse: for ye have robbed me, even this whole nation.*

✠ Mal 3:8 10 *Bring ye all the tithes into the storehouse, that there may be meat in mine house, and prove me now herewith, saith the Lord of hosts, if I will not open you the windows of heaven, and pour you out a blessing, that there shall not be room enough to receive it.*

In the book of Malachi chapter three, the main reason men of God in those days ask people to bring tithes into the house of God, is so that the priest can get paid. When the priest prays for you, he gets paid for doing the work of the Lord, not just because he/she prayed for you. He/she is spending his/her time with you. If you want to go the extra mile just give an offering only if you cannot yet afford to pay your tithes yet.

However, this book is about how lies can destroy lives, if care is not taken. We need to watch and pray as believers that we don't allow the devil's children, to keep us away from the will of God.

The will of God is that we know God and his ways, through reading the Holy bible, his word, so that we can please God.

Like my other two non fiction books inspired by my faith. Some elements of this book is about, to Have a free will, and not being manipulated into doing things that you as an individual don't like. Unlike "Polygamy if God wills it, it should not be a form of Slavery then," Which was mainly about avoiding exploitation in a polygamous home. Likewise, I want you to again be set free from the bondage of what the bible describes as the children of the devil. Plus the devil himself. The biblical references in this book, are there to help you see with ease my explanations.

Digressing, So friends in the Lord, no matter what you are going through in life, whether you feel that God has abandoned you or not, do not let anything make you to renounce God, or turn your back from God. God is good, in our ups and downs in life, God is good always be positive. I know sometime it's like God is nowhere to be found, but I believe if we hold on, we will have the best opportunity in life, in ...

.......Heaven, when we are old and we die. Some things in life are a nonsense and the ingredients.

Also, as much as God is holy, he cares about our welfare too. To be clean and moderate. I would add that you also be careful not to mix bright deep colours together with whites and light colours, don't assume it won't dye without always test washing it as you might have forgotten, e.g. a red top, without testing it first as its colour might run and mess up your other clothes,...

.... so do the test the first time you buy the clothes.

During my daily bible study I came across some scriptures.

KJV Numbers 8:5 "And the Lord spake unto Moses, saying,"

Numbers 8:6 "Take the Levites from among the children of Isreal, and cleanse them." Numbers 8:7 "And thus thou shalt do unto them, to cleanse them: Sprinkle water of purifying upon them, and let them shave all their flesh, and let them wash their clothes, and so make themselves clean."

Numbers 8:8 "Then let them take a young bullock with his meat offering, even fine flour mingled with oil, and another young bullock shalt thou take for a sin offering."

This scripture explains how God want the consecrated children of his chosen people to be clean physically as well spiritually. But in the era of Moses the prophet, killing of animals were used as an atonement, for sin, but now the blood of Jesus cleanses us of our sins, so that we are not cut off from God.

The last scripture is how God instructed those who serve him in the temple not to wear clothes that will cause them to sweat.

KJV Ezekiel 44:15 "But the priest the Levites, the sons of Zadok, that kept the charge of my sanctuary when the children of Israel went astray from me, they shall come near to me to minister unto me, and they shall stand before me to offer unto me the fat and the blood, saith the Lord God:"

KJV Ezekiel 44:17 "And it shall come to pass, that when they enter in at the gates of the inner courts, they shall be clothed with linen garments; and no wool shall come upon them, whilst they minister in the gates of the inner courts, and within.

✠ *In conclusion, one thing I have discovered about God is that, he has the power to tell people for example if he wants someone to be a nurse or a...*

....*childminder, or to work in the ministry, be a designer, an engineer, a Dr, Lawyer, pharmacist etc. etc. he Could tell them, but instead he won't, he wants us to try to figure out what is our purpose in life, and why the individual's life is yielding some unwanted weaknesses and all the negative energies that occurs in an individual's life, the individual, trying to figure all these out.*

But the book of Jeremiah KJV 29:11 says, "For I know the thoughts that I think toward you, saith the Lord, thoughts of peace, and not of evil, to give you an expected end." So where is that expected end; and where is that peace of mind, because my joy aint with the devil, it's with God, God will give you peace of mind, when you are worrying whether your man is with your best friend or a successful younger family member. Also, when you are sad; and that because of your vulnerability of being a deep sleeper. When you pray God will answer you, he is good all the time.

This vulnerability can lead some people, even men and women of God to introduce you to Polygamy through not naturally stimulated but unnaturally stimulated sexual urges via Aphrodisiac Viagra, don't do it, because polygamy is a plan of the devil to make you into a sex tool.

Because God is Holy so if I don't have a man to myself, then I ought to be holy as well, do my job and get a real job and concentrate on this, why not. If he wants me to do Polygamy, I will obey Him, but it has to be God who says we should do it, plus I need to consent as well, be in agreement with God, in order to do the Polygamy. I am not trying to be horrible to anyone, I am just asking why should this be the case? Polygamy in itself is not wrong, but only wrong, when you are being forced into it, or deceived into it, in the case of deception, it should be against the law, people need to consent to it ◯ -!!!-

I think the police force in England are not very good, reason why is that, some of them are bullies and could allow a witch Dr to spike your food or drink with Viagra/aphrodisiac.

Also, be careful of a so called friend that you let come do sleep over, possibly could, molest you in the sleep at night, If it were possible.

So be careful who you let into your home and you call a friend, _As I don't think the police will be able to do anything about it, if you cannot prove it....._

Also, in broad day light, some bad; and not good witch Dr's has a certificate to practice. I feel it's the same all around the world I don't know, but this is not the point, all I know is that I think the police force in England are not very good.

If someone wanted you dead, all they have to do is come to your face, to show you what they can do to you if you don't comply.

These hypocrites, so called safe guarding workers are all evil. who I believe allow, witch Doctor's, or a person, to spike your drink or food, with.........

................aphrodisiac or Viagra, so that you can get sexual urges, that will lead you to be sleeping with a man that you might not be in love with.

Why don't they come to your face if they want you dead, they wait until after one child, block your womb thereafter so you cannot have more children. But then, before you know it, you can be sleeping around under the influence of their aphrodisiac, you may or may not get sexually transmitted disease, then you may find yourself in the heavens, eating pan cake plus singing hallelujah to God.

Also, if you are vulnerable, be careful what friends you keep, or let to do sleep over, so they don't molest you in the sleep. If the police and your family, were doing their job properly in the first place, you would be protected.

Romans 6 : 23 <u>"For the wages of sin is death ; but the gift of God is eternal life through Jesus Christ our Lord."</u>

I WOULD R ATHER BE DE AD, I WOULDN'T LE AVE MY CHILD WITH THEM EITHER.

Basically if you are not in a relationship with the man you love, <u>then maybe you can go join the Coventry</u> or just simply be holy all by yourself, as like God commanded, but the aphrodisiac and Viagra won't let you will it? They want to clone people into relationships that suits them, that is wrong; and I personally will not let someone take me for a ride nor to be controlling me in this way.

I'm sorry but keep telling yourself you have not yet found a husband, some of the men they give you are only coming to see what's good in your life before they get rid of you so the next selfish can come in, even some of these same men, might not even be your type to start with. They don't know God nor do they have the fear of a God in heaven, they might replace you I'm so sorry for you. I'm talking from experience.

Some men even go to the extent to say they believe in God and go to church, (pardon me for saying that-the worst people are those men who go to church). In fact some would say men will be men, but I want you to understand something carefully, people go to church all the time and say they are a true Christian, whilst in actual fact, they are not true Christians, as they are not grounded in the love of God, so just because someone goes to church doesn't mean you should have a high expectation of them, be careful not to get your heart broken, don't judge, but don't expect everyone to be perfect in the church don't be put off to date men/women in the church, I'm just saying they could break your heart that's all. A TRUE CHRISTIAN MAN OR WOMAN WON'T HURT YOUR FEELINGs, NOR WILL THEY USE YOU FOR SEX. Even the bible says, [beware of wolves in sheep's clothing], Some claim to be true Christians, but are not.

K J V Romans 6:14-23

14 *"For sin shall not have dominion over you : for ye are not under the law, but under grace."*

15 *"What then? shall we sin, because we are not under the law, but under grace? God forbid."*

16 *"Know ye not, that to whom ye yield yourselves servants to obey, his servants ye are to whom ye obey ; whether of sin unto death, or of obedience unto righteousness?"*

17 *"But God be thanked, that ye were the servants of sin, but ye have obeyed from the heart that form of doctrine which was delivered you."*

18 *"Being then made free from sin, ye became the servants of righteousness."*

19 *"I speak after the manner of men because of the infirmity of your f lesh : for as ye have yielded your members servants to uncleanness and to iniquity unto iniquity; even so now yield your members servants to righteousness unto holiness."*

20 *"For when ye were the servants of sin, ye were free from righteousness."*

21 *"What fruit had ye then in those things whereof ye are now ashamed? for the end of those things is death."*

22 *"But now being made free from sin, and become servants to God, ye have your fruit unto holiness, and the end everlasting life."*

23 *"For the wages of sin is death; but the gift of God is eternal life through Jesus Christ our Lord."*

You can sleep with descent men and still catch something. So get yourself checked. Flipping Twats !!!

I think if a man loves you, he would understand your situation, and would do what it takes to trust you; and get to know you, before judging you.

HEAVEN KNOWS you are supposed to be Holy like your father in heaven is,.......

..... whether you want to stay celebrate, meaning like to just abstain from sex or if you want to wait for the right man to come along before becoming sexually active!!! Rom 6 :19 "I speak after the manner of men because of the infirmity of your f lesh: for as ye have yielded your members servants to uncleanness and to iniquity unto iniquity; even so now yield your members servants to *righteousness unto holiness.*"

> Psalm 29 :2 *Give unto the Lor d the glory due unto his name ; worship the Lord in the beauty of holiness.*

KJV Psalm 29:1 Give unto the LoRd, O ye mighty, give unto the

LoRd glory and strength.

Psalm 29:2 *Give unto the Lord the glory due unto his name ; worship the Lord in the beauty of holiness.*

Psalm 29:3 The voice of the LoRd is upon the waters: the God of glory thundereth: the LoRd is upon many waters.

Psalm 29:4 The voice of the LoRd is powerful; the voice of the LoRd is full of majesty.

Psalm 29:5 The voice of the LoRd breaketh the cedars; yea, the LoRd breaketh the cedars of Lebanon.

Psalm 29: 6 He maketh them also to skip like a calf; Lebanon and Sirion like a young unicorn.

Psalm 29:7 The voice of the LoRd divideth the f lames of fire.

Psalm 29:8 The voice of the LoRd shaketh the wilderness; the LoRd shaketh the wilderness of Kadesh.

Psalm 29:9 The voice of the LoRd maketh the hinds to calve, and discovereth the forests: and in his temple doth every one speak of his glory.

Psalm 29:10 The LoRd sitteth upon the f lood; yea, the LoRd sitteth King for ever.

> Psalm 29:11 The LoRd will give strength unto his people; the LoRd will bless his people with peace.

Going out with old men is your choice are you under the inf luence of Viagra?

If you want to date an older man, the choice is yours but I don't like the fact that he is above 50 have spent most of his life doing what he has done, then he wants you. But who am I to judge, what works for me, might not work for you, vice versa, so think what you want to do then. If God says you r husband is an older man above 50 so be it then.

But I'd advice, go for someone 6 years younger or 7 years older than you

Female sterilisation, condoms

🕐 *Sterilisation*

I used to think sterilisation was a good thing and that even contraceptives were good. But I just *now* feel that these things are evil.

God made you a woman, it should be under your control not to or to have a baby. *Meaning, I am not sure of the medical principle of this,* but I don't think that people have a period without using medication to stimulate this.

Likewise, men aren't to come until they are given medication to come. So, we can then see clearly that contraceptives methods are evil. Such as, e.g., <u>*IUS SHORT FOR INTR AUTERINE SYSTEM IN THE MEDICAL TERM*</u> *coils, contraceptive pills, sterilisation getting your tubes tied or cut, vasectomy are all evil, I think so. unless for crucial and serious medical reasons, I don't agree with these methods of contraceptives.*

<u>*BUT Abortive PILLS ARE A PERSONAL CHOICE!!!*</u>

If a man doesn't come at the wrong time, the woman doesn't need her period to f lush things out of her, to the point of pregnancy.

Out of all the contraceptive methods, it is gruesome to have a females fallopian tube cut off or tied, or even to remove her womb in the name of taking contraceptive measures, this is a demonic attack from the pit of hell and the workers of iniquity who are not only suited and booted for this use, but are bloody paid for it.

Condoms are okay, if used appropriately.

I have come to realize that, when a child is born, there are medication designed by God for the purpose to make the young boy to have male features, vice versa the young girl to have female features. Even a flat stomach can be relevant, then definitely, your shoe size is important like Pinocchio.

I think for short to average height boys (maximum size should be shoe size 8 if tall size 10)

For girls, short to average, or tall height (maximum size should be shoes size6) Or if they gave an average height female size5 feet, we'd get the point a lot faster. <u>Because they have always got the flipping excuses. Plus they are selfish people.</u>

Readers, don't let anyone deceive you that a short person 5 foot 3inches, with size 7 feet has inherited the genetics of the male side as men are the ones who tend to have long feet.

Because the same genetics that gave size 7 feet, can also give size 5 feet...

...... I'm not complaining, just saying, some people are selfish Twats. Try not to get upset over long feet. Long feet, you can still tolerate. Honestly I don't know why they're trying to make life difficult for you as a female, just for no apparent reason.

God bless, Take care.

Because, anything other than this, is from the evil jealous one, plus that is time wasting. God himself is jealous; plus will not allow the mockery of his children or his people.

I now think, that selfish people, should replenish the earth and reproduce it. If we were all to form a Koo, <u>IN LINE WITH ThE WiLL OF GOD,</u> to leave them to it. How would they like it O?

Try to make things snappy in anything you do if you can, but whatever requires patience, take your time and do it well, as whatever is worth doing, is worth doing well.

<u>A whore is a ditch and a strange woman is a narrow pit</u>

New Living Translation Proverbs 23:27 "A prostitute is a deep pit; an adulterous woman is treacherous. "

> KJ V Proverbs 23 :27 "For a whore *is* a deep ditch; and a strange woman *is* a narrow pit." <u>28</u> "She also lieth in wait as *for* a prey, and increaseth the transgressors among men." <u>29</u> "Who hath woe? who hath sorrow? who hath contentions? who hath babbling? who hath wounds without cause? who hath redness of eyes?" <u>30</u> "They that tarry long at the wine; they that go to seek mixed wine."

The way I see it is that a prostitute can be a sex worker if she wishes, but she gets sex and get paid for it as well.

This business can be in two ways as well accessed in two ways, a working female, pays a male sex worker for sex, which I think is no better than women selling their bodies, though women are more sensitive to infections this way round if the female is the sex worker.

I don't like either Male or female prostitution let alone with more than 4 sex partners triangle.

I.e., It attracts problems, if one Male prostitute is involved with 3 women, vice versa, if one woman a prostitute, sleeps with 3 Male costumers on different days, then, the women or men you're involved with could try to harass you later on in life, the less customers you are involved with the better.

But it'll be better to avoid these things all together, prostitution whoremonger job is a problem, not to talk of a sin.

Note, Since you've prayed, fasted and worshiped God, still the urge doesn't go away.

Then, if it is the case that you have no man that you are actually interested in, to have to yourself. **DO NOT GET** *a male sex worker to have sex with him,* **to be paying him, till you find the right man then, this is wrong, but the choice is yours.**

ARE YOU ON VIAGRA OR APHRODISIAC or something?

I repeat plus reiterate, that both Male as well Female prostitution, are both a sin!!! I ask again, *ARE YOU ON VIAGRA OR APHRODISIAC?*

If a man were to be divorced and single, or never been married before and single, he can get involved in…

…….POLY-A-MORY … …relationship, that would be his choice, but note this is wrong I don't like it. WHY CAN'T THE SINGLE FEMALES, GO FOR SOMEONE who is actually available, <u>or might even BE a younger person than themselves, please?</u>

<u>Why does a married man have to be sleeping with side females, then they pay the married man, an affordable fee!</u>

<u>That is indirect male *prostitution isn't it? A married man who is having numerous girlfriends, plus concubines, will not be able to look after his wife properly, nor care for if it is, the case, his only wife. Because of his other MISSES.*</u>

<u>If you, the only main wife at the time finds out, if you wish, you may tell him, to go pick one of his loose women, or O's, to make as a new main wife, Then as usual, to continue with the rest of his side chicks, well see how that other</u>

new wife, will like that. Treat unto others as you'd like for yourself.

Furthermore, *him doing this is cheating on his wife.*

Then one of his loose women could seduce him to leave the main wife. So A No No to this arrangement please!

Digressing, be warned.

I like my perfume to smell nice, but there is a difference, between nice perfume and such thing as seducing perfume. Be warned.

Hence, so, don't go to a female's home alone. Vice versa, don't go to a male's home alone. Unless you are either going to be faithful if he/she tries to seduce you, OR ONLY Go ALONE, if you trust that he / she won't try to seduce you.

It's like, are you kidding me right now? I repeat, what are those single women doing with the married man in the first place. Cannot they find their own man, even a younger person. ARE THEY ON APHRODISIAC OR VIAGRA? Because they don't want to be in control of their sexual urge, are they on Viagra, go marry an available person, even if younger than you, if not SORRY, you cannot SHARE a married man unless you are, ALL plus NO MORE THAN, THE second wife, PLUS ALL CONSENTING ADULTS HAVE TO CONSENT, PERIOD!!!

I'm telling you, trying different women will mess that man up, he won't be able to focus on his main wife, if it is his only wife, she might even die from the stress of neglect in the relationship. It is not his responsibility, to be sexing other women, they need their own man o,

<u>whatever it takes, even a younger person, so be it! *Leave happy married couples alone please.*</u>

When a man is married, the law says that he can have girlfriends if he wants. But Polygamy is Illegal. I don't even know why that is allowed, but Polygamy with maximum two women, is Illegal.

The problem with a married man being allowed to have girlfriend(s) as opposed to polygamy, is that in that type of relationship, the female could leave and ruin the relationship of the man and his wife.

However, I prefer polygamy with a close relative than family friend or than even a good stranger, plus, with all adult participants, consenting.

At least in a polygamous relationship, there is commitment, Plus loyalty. I don't like either of the two, but if you are going to be doing all that, then Polygamy is way better. I don't even think Polygamy is a sin, I just don't like the problem that comes with it. So best do it with a close relative only, not even a so called nice stranger, or family friend. With all consenting parties to actually consent to the act. Anything outside this box, is violation.

If either or both the married man and the new proposed female partner, is or are caught lying to the main wife. The man or both should be prosecuted with lenient fines, or even locked up in Jail, if either or both are caught lying to the main wife, because they can harm with their lies, because, she need to be aware of what her man is up to please!

Wifey, IF YOU CATCH YOUR MAN LYING AND CHEATING, IF HE WON'T LEAVE THAT SELFISH home wrecker ALONE. First of all, stay in the marriage but don't allow him touch you anymore. With prayers, that hopefully he will come to his senses; and leave those loose and selfish, females alone. However, if he forcefully kicks you out of the matrimonial home, and not responding to your kind and patient gestures, as well secret prayers, even if you shout out when he is in the other room, that is still your secret prayers. As you may become, prayerfully, aggressive, when distressed. <u>SO THEN</u>, if he forcefully kicks you out of the matrimonial home, you may want to consider divorcing him.

Then, MAYBE YOU SHOULD LEAVE THEM TO IT THEN. Go for someone who is available, or that might, even be a younger person than you please wifey, if the man won't stop his cheating.

Otherwise I don't like this option you sell your body for sex, so you don't have to commit until you get a Mr. Right, or you go with any Tom, dick and Harry, that you are not in Love with ; and live a...

.... very angry, miserable or bitter life. It's not funny I'm telling you this now, I'd rather be on my own if I don't get a man that I love.

But my Question still stands, are you under a sexual drug that is causing your sex drive to come on, or are you just naturally looking for sex ?

<u>**Or are you on Aphrodisiac or Viagra or something?**</u>

I reiterate, WHY, do the 3 or 4 females want to be disturbing a married man that they are not in a Polygamous relationship with.

I ask again, <u>Or are you on Aphrodisiac or Viagra?</u>

<u>It's not very exciting being in a Polygamous relationship with just two women, but 3 or four, that is crazy.</u>

<u>I think 2 females may be certified in a polygamous relationship, but, ABOVE 2 women in a polygamous relationship should be banned.</u>

Otherwise I don't like this option you sell your body for sex, so you don't have to commit until you get a Mr right, or you go with any Tom, dick and Harry, that you are not in Love with ; and live a…

……. very angry, miserable or bitter life. It's not funny I'm telling you this now, I'd rather be on my own if I don't get a man that I love.

But my Question still stands, are you under a sexual drug that is causing your sex drive to come on, or are you just naturally looking for sex ?

Aphrodisiac or Viagra?

<u>Adam and eve with the apple on the tree don't touch a vulnerable person</u>

Those using witchcraft to do evil, are wrong and should be banned. Why do they have the right to practice what they do to harm others/ to embarrass them?

I think that those witches that don't use their witchcraft on others or don't use it at all, should be left alone.

But those using witchcraft to do evil, if caught, should be banned.

In the bible, pharaoh's magicians performed magic, but never used it on people.

Like wise Moses did his own performance as well. I will reiterate this later on again.

For example it is evil for a witch Dr to give an individual hair in the wrong place to humiliate the individual, or to give then (<u>a syndrome (a Martin syndrome) - bumps at parts or all over your body or skin), cancer of any sort and the likes of these,</u> or to give the individual sex drive secretly like aphrodisiac/Viagra, in order for the person to become promiscuous, you'll be lucky if you don't sleep with the wrong man and catch a sexually transmitted disease or you'll be lucky, if you don't catch something.

I think that those witches that don't use their witchcraft on others or don't use it at all, should be left alone. But those using witchcraft to do evil, if caught, should be banned. In the bible, pharaoh's magicians performed magic, but never used it on people. Like wise Moses did his own performance as well.

I feel, that sometimes, I think the witch Dr make a wrong decision, when he / she chooses to embarrass an individual, why not approach the person in the open so they may have to say their last prayers...

<u>God is the God of light and does things in an open manner, or is God playing games with vulnerable adults ? As it stands those in Authority certainly are.</u>

Also, all good and perfect gifts comes from the Lord of lights, not the god of darkness !

........<u>whilst some ordinary people and witch Drs may do more than embarrass you, they are just plain evil,</u> when they can take your life away; and are practicing hardcore voodoo.

When once again, when the witch Dr, *<u>might be allowed</u>*, to spike your drink with aphrodisiac or Viagra, when *<u>authorities permits this possibly</u>*, then, when the private landlord, probably has spare keys to your f lat, then lets the witch Dr into the property. Also, I'm not saying this is the case, but even if it is the case, don't worry, they probably won't go into your f lat without your permission. If it were to be a council property it might be different I don't know.

Also, in a public place, your drink could get spiked, so be cautious of this too, *not only* of private Landlords, witch Dr's and private accommodations/ council properties.

Then, watch who you sleep with, because if you sleep with the wrong person, you could get sexually transmitted disease. You could sleep with the right people and still catch something, so get tested. Aphrodisiac or Viagra can lead to promiscuity, when, in your right mind as a child of God you know fornication is a sin. I'm not saying all sexual urges are stemmed from a love drug such as Aphrodisiac or Viagra, *but I am just saying be cautious of what might be going on around you, as why should someone who prays so hard like you ; and believes in God, should be under the temptation of sexual urges, if not that it might not be natural feelings, but topped or inf- luenced by a sexual drug like aphrodisiac or Viagra.*

Naturally if a male and a female come together, they will definitely get turned on, but I think once you leave each other, you could control the urge. So be careful. Also, don't worry if you suspect you are under the inf luence of Viagra or aphrodisiac, don't fight with anyone, just keep trusting God to Perfect all negative things in your life.

Also, if it were possible, *you could get Molested in the sleep, if you're a deep sleeper,* so be careful who you let into your life and your home, as so called friends could betray you.

1 Samuel 26:8-9……..This shows that vulnerable people are at the mercy of those around them.

8 "Abishai said to David, "Today God has delivered your enemy into your hands. Now let me pin him to the ground with one thrust of the spear; I won't strike him twice."

9 "But David said to Abishai, "Don't destroy him! Who can lay a hand on the LORD's anointed and be guiltless?"

Where there is love you will last, even if you are vulnerable. Meaning if you have a good man by your side, you will be just fine.

Maybe like Adam and Eve with the apple on the tree they shouldn't touch a vulnerable person. Should they touch the vulnerable person, then maybe they should carry them along with what is going on.

Romans 8 :1 "There is therefore now no condemnation to them which are in Christ Jesus, who walk not after the f lesh, but after the Spirit."

First of all I want you to be aware of something, <u>I used to get angry at</u> <u>God for my mishaps/mistakes made in life, bad</u> decisions, though I am now not angry at God for the temptations I face, neither am I saying that God is bad, but I am just trying to make a way of escape if you like out of a difficult situation. Also, trying to make a way to manage temptations as a believer or as an infidel- a non believer of Christ. Remember God is sovereign, and he makes things perfect in his own time.

I will bless the God who gives and takes away.

Why paying for sex might be your best bet, <u>meaning you don't sell your</u> <u>body to be an escort,</u> but you get a job; and pay a man who you know is a sex worker to sleep with you also I'm not trying to be funny or anything like that, sometimes you have to do what you have to do until God intervenes.

The reason I say this is because,......

.... if I have tried so hard to restrain myself from fornication, sex outside marriage as a follower of Christ, but yet still, the power of aphrodisiac or Viagra, which may have been spiked into your food or drink when you leave your home or in a public place, then the odds are against you. It's up to you, think about it.

You may end up needing to pay for sex. I don't know about you, but after thinking about my life, several silly billys are after me just because they want to give me the impression that I am their wife.

They give you a comfort zone, you relax and think you have it good when all they are just doing is taking you for a ride, you also give them a blow job in return, like he is just using you for sex and wasting your time in the marriage.

SORRY ABOUT BEING EXPLICIT but it's what I think to be true. Even though you don't love him it was the sex drug that lead you to it, so then, the day they'll give you cancer and terminate you so the next <u>selfish</u> can step in, you'll probably find yourself, in the heaven eating pancake *with God/ or singing hallelujah to God. <u>SO, FINDERS KEEPERS, LOSER WEEPERS.</u>*

Don't get me wrong marriage is good, but I don't think you are really married, when it is with a man you don't love, it's like he is just using you for sex and wasting your time.

I don't know how to approach this, but I shouldn't be forced into a sexual relation with a man just because someone thinks they will have control over me, a witch Dr whom the police certifies to drug you, so you can be going with men, that, in your right senses will not normally go with, that is Bloody disgusting.

<u>I don't know about you, but I wouldn't want a commitment from that, I'd rather pay for sex if this is a legal option, until if I meet a Mr right, in a way, this is my way of REBELLING against being controlled against my wish. Or go on a dating site or something. The choice is Yours, if the witch Dr were to behave his or herself, he /she would stop making you to get sexual urges under the inf luence of Viagra /aphrodisiac.</u>

<u>If they have any conscience, they'd iron things out with you in the open.</u>

Then there is the issues of being proposed to by several men in the UK,....

.... these silly billies in UK, but where is the sense in that, how many men are interested in you pls, plus why are they all single at the same time.

ALL after one thing to use and dump you. Why won't the f lipping men take No for an answer, <u>I mean the ones I'm not interested in out of the no. of guys that like me three.</u>

If I were the police, I would put restrictive orders on men who are harassing women for a hand in a relationship they are not interested in, if this law is breached then they can look into arresting the man. This is harassment, the legal system all over the world especially here in the UK is so corrupt, any Tom Dick and harry can molest you, even whilst awake, can still try to molest you and f lipping get away with it in the sight of a Holy God. How can they just put their dirty filthy hands on you.

You can try to remain celebrate before commitment, also before committing to a relationship, you need to check each other's bodies, because I have heard of situation here in the UK, when the man's balls looked injured and the woman had to leave him. *So be careful!!*

Still be careful, if you are a virgin check each other before marriage. Also, do a sexually transmitted disease test. Because you don't want to catch Aids / HIV, please keep your virginity.

Sex should be a choice not a forceful act. God himself said, "I place bEfore you life and death choose life that you may live". This is to say God doesn't force he advises. So therefore, any sexual urge leading to sexual immorality is not of God, perhaps you are under the inf luence of a sex drug, it could be natural, it could be because of a sexual stimulant I don't know, this might be the reason you might be craving sex.

If this is the case, God will never force you to do polygamy, it would be your choice to do this too. If they wanted you to be a Nanny or child minder, we'd get the point a lot faster, you'd do your job and get paid, why do you have to do polygamy, to be sleeping with someone else's husband, if you don't like this. Don't get me wrong, polygamy has it's uses, and there is a time and place for everything; and everything should be in it's place. God bless.

But never the less, calm down and don't go getting angry, assuming that someone has spiked your drink with a sex drug, to the point of hitting someone in authority, because they will either,

1. *Section you,*
2. *Or Prosecute you,*

So, calm down, since you cannot prove it and keep praying to God that he will help you to get better and to be in control of your life, I'm afraid, that is the only weapon you' ll have, prayer is the way to breakthrough.

Also, then there is the big HIV test thing, I usually take men's' word for it that they are clear of the virus, but really you really shouldn't be having sex with a man if he doesn't get the test first. Also, don't use rubber with any man you don't trust, as they might go too fast and the rubber might go deep in you. Also, condom can split at the side, so be careful you have been warned.

Also if a woman says no to a man, whether the man is to be pitied or has some sort of vulnerability, then nO IS NO, the police or anyone in authority do not have any right to cajole, persuade, coerce, threaten or psychologically threaten, another human being into being in a relationship with someone they are not interested in, either by law, or by Viagra? If they just want to be on their own instead, or to find someone else.

KJV (King James Version)

Hosea 1:1 "The word of the LORD that came unto Hosea, the son of Beeri, in the days of Uzziah, Jotham, Ahaz, and Hezekiah, kings of Judah, and in the days of Jeroboam the son of Joash, king of Israel."

Hosea 1:2 "The beginning of the word of the LORD by Hosea. And the LORD said to Hosea, Go, take unto thee a wife of whoredoms and children of whoredoms: for the land hath committed great whoredom, departing from the LORD."

Hosea 1:3 "So he went and took Gomer the daughter of Diblaim; which conceived, and bare him a son."

Hosea 1:4 "And the LORD said unto him, Call his name Jezreel; for yet a little while, and I will avenge the blood of Jezreel upon the house of Jehu, and will cause to cease the kingdom of the house of Israel."

Hosea 1:5 "And it shall come to pass at that day, that I will break the bow of Israel, in the valley of Jezreel."

NIV (New International Version)

Hosea 1:1 "The word of the LORD that came to Hosea son of Beeri during the reigns of Uzziah, Jotham, Ahaz and Hezekiah, kings of Judah, and during the reign of Jeroboam son of Jehoash[a] king of Israel:"

Hosea's Wife and Children

Hosea 1:2 "When the LORD began to speak through Hosea, the LORD said to him, "Go, marry a promiscuous woman and have children with her, for like an adulterous wife this land is guilty of unfaithfulness to the LORD." Hosea 1:3 "So he married Gomer daughter of Diblaim, and she conceived and bore him a son."

Hosea 1:4 "Then the LORD said to Hosea, "Call him Jezreel, because I will soon punish the house of Jehu for the massacre at Jezreel, and I will put an end to the kingdom of Israel. Hosea 1:5 In that day I will break Israel's bow in the Valley of Jezreel."

Hosea 1: 6 "Gomer conceived again and gave birth to a daughter. Then the LORD said to Hosea, "Call her Lo-Ruhamah (which means "not loved"), for I will no longer show love to Israel, that I should at all forgive them." Hosea 1:7 "Yet I will show love to Judah; and I will save them—not by bow, sword or battle, or by horses and horsemen, but I, the LORD their God, will save them."

Hosea 1: 8 "After she had weaned Lo-Ruhamah, Gomer had another son."

Hosea 1:9 "Then the LORD said, "Call him Lo-Ammi (which means "not my people"), for you are not my people, and I am not your God."[b

In this bible passage we notice that there appears to be a lot of worshiping of other Gods, idolatry probably, going on in the land in the first place ; and people turning away from God doing all manner of evil, having no faith in the God of Abraham, Isaac and Jacob, in other words, the God of Moses and Jesus Christ. So God had compassion on the land of Israel, instead of rejecting them completely. So, he told Hosea to go marry an unbeliever, since faithlessness against the God of Moses, was rampant in the land already. I don't understand this scripture very well, but this is my own little understanding of a loving and forgiving God. The name Lo-Ruhamah, which means God will no longer show love to Israel, probably because if they don't change their ways of whoredom, then he will keep his distance from them.

KJV John 4:7 -19

KJV John 4:7 There cometh a woman of Samaria to draw water: Jesus saith unto her, Give me to drink.

KJV John 4:8 (For his disciples were gone away unto the city to buy meat.)

KJV John 4 :9 Then saith the woman of Samaria unto him, How is it that thou, being a Jew, askest drink of me, which am a woman of Samaria? for the Jews have no dealings with the Samaritans.

KJV John 4:10 *Jesus answered and said unto her, If thou knewest the gift of God, and who it is that saith to thee, Give me to drink ; thou wouldest have asked of him, and he would have given thee living water.*

KJV John 4 :11 The woman saith unto him, Sir, thou hast nothing to draw with, and the well is deep: from whence then hast thou that living water?

KJV John 4:12 Art thou greater than our father Jacob, which gave us the well, and drank thereof himself, and his children, and his cattle?

KJ V John 4 :13 Jesus answered and said unto her, Whosoever drinketh of this water shall thirst again:

KJV John 4 :14 *But whosoever drinketh of the water that I shall give him shall never thirst ; but the water that I shall give him shall be in him a well of water springing up into everlasting life.*

KJV John 4 :15 The woman saith unto him, Sir, give me this water, that I thirst not, neither come hither to draw.

KJV John 4:16 Jesus saith unto her, Go, call thy husband, and come hither.

KJV John 4 :17 The woman answered and said, I have no husband. Jesus said unto her, Thou hast well said, I have no husband:

KJV John 4 :18 *For thou hast had five husbands ; and he whom thou now hast is not thy husband : in that saidst thou truly.*

KJV John 4 :19 *The woman saith unto him, Sir, I perceive that thou art a prophet.*

In this bible passages, the person of Jesus, (depicts – shows) three things, that those who believe in Christ, believe in a:

- *Compassionate,*
- *prophetic God*
- *A God* who is also the God of everlasting life.

The men as well women of God who truly believe in God, can prophecy, when they hear from God. This is why I don't like a church, where the clerg y both male or female, cannot prophecy. Also, before you can trust what he / she says, you need to be grounded in the relevant church to form a (rapport- relationship) with the man or woman of God.

Songs

1. I want to be holy unto yo u

I want to be holy unto you,
I want to be worth of your name; and as I live this life for you, I
declare your majesty and King.

2. I behold yo u

I behold you, most holy one,
I behooold you as the lamb on the
throne, As I worship you, in reverent
fear,
I behold you,
Jesus the
lamb.

3. Draw me close - (Michael w. Smith)

[Verse]
Draw me close to You
Never let me go
I lay it all down again
To hear You say that I'm Your friend
You are my desire
No one else will do
'Cause nothing else can take Your
place To feel the warmth of Your
embrace Help me find the way
Bring me back to You

[Chorus]
You're all I want
You're all I've ever needed
You're all I want
Help me know You are near

Also, I want to clear the air about something, in my book, "Polygamy if God wills it, it should not be a form of slavery then !"

I mentioned that my ex husband's sperm smells like Omega 3, well I lied as I was trying to protect my self-image as a saint, actually, his sperm smells normal that is my Ex husbands sperm smells normal, because after we separated, I dated other guys.

It was a Caucasian white guy I dated after my marriage that his sperm smelt a bit like omega 3 capsules oil. This is just to set the records straight.

Though, I am now open to the idea of prostitution in the sense that I won't judge people who do it, as I don't know why they do what they do.

On the other hand, prostitution is not good, as if the Prostitute & the man paying the prostitute, are not on Viagra, then why are they doing it why do they need sex.

Also, if in the business, it can be bad if the man rapes you to give you Anus sex if this is not what you want for yourself.

I repeat, it can be bad if the man rapes you to give you anus sex, as even in broad day light, I think and assume or guess that, the legal system in the UK condoles and allows sex workers to get away with cold blooded assault in which case some could get away with cold blooded murder without a gun to their hand.

As even in broad day light to try to infect a woman, this could lead to her getting an operation which could take her life from her. Rape is a serious offence, but criminals have their way to get away with it in the system, because the law surrounding sex workers is not <u>stringent</u>, strict *or tight enough. They take things with levity, when some men are just there to go to an Harlot, to contaminate women, by raping them during sexual intercourse by giving anus sex, IHOPE THE SA ME DICK THEY PUT IN HER aNUS IS NOT WHAT THEY WILL PUT IN HER VAGINA.*

I think, tighter laws have to be put in place as to what is agreed when a man pays for sex, If the woman says no to certain things like No to anus sex then a breach in this should lead to police custody and arrest.

Mind you prostitutes have it easy, they have sex and get paid for it, but it is also a way to get sex if you don't want commitment with a man until you find a Mr right; and get paid for it, so have fun. Why are they doing it, what led them to prostitution, as if it is not <u>*so called natural urges,*</u> then are they under the possible inf luence of Viagra/aphrodisiac, if this *is the case, then prostitution is wrong.*

But I am serious about anus sex, I don't like it even if you are a prostitute, doesn't mean you should be forced into Anus sex, if you don't like it, the police need to put restrictions on this or f lipping stop the Viagra.

In the UK a woman is being harassed to go out with a man she is not interested in in fact two men; and she believes the Police are insinuating threats to send someone to give her anus sex if she doesn't comply, as the men are still harassing her.

If she complains to them, they'll only refer her to the psychiatric team, who will give her more drugs. Then, to possibly provoke her because she feels she is under the inf luence of aphrodisiac, so she might get frustrated and angry and possibly hit someone then e n d u p i n ps yc hi at r i c hospital or even prison. Just because she doesn't want to be controlled in this way.

This is sexual harassment from those in Authority and the two men in question.

Likewise, a woman is not suppose to use her period until given medication, so that she can get pregnant. This is a speculation a guess. <u>So any form of IUS SHORT FOR INTRAUTERINE SYSTEM IN THE MEDICAL TERMs</u> contraceptive wire or plastics coils, inserted in you or a sterilisation, a female having her fallopian tube tied or cut up, vasectomy for men, all of these acts are not necessary and are therefore evil from the pit of hell, sex lies and your soul, you'll be lucky if you survive the operation.

<u>These are the sort of lies, that can lead to death. Sex lies and <u>your</u> <u>soul.</u></u>

Can a loving God instruct you, instead of instructing the Clergies men or women of God about your life please ? This is not to be rude, it's just a question.

That is just some of the things that could happen BECAUSE YOU ARE AT THE MERCY OF THOSE AROUND YOU.

The enemy, the devil might use devilish professionals, to try to slow down, the flow of your menstruation also known as your period, because they are evil plain and simple.

Furthermore, [the enemy, has come to steal to kill and to destroy, but Jesus said, he has come to give you life, and to give life more abundantly], John 10:10 KJV, that is what him and his followers do.

The enemy would want to <u>slow down,</u> the flow of your menstruation also known as your period, because they are evil plain and simple. In order to form clogs. That is probably how you get diagnosed with womb problem such as <u>Fibroid.</u>

I just want to add, and to make the young novice know and to be aware, that, you're womb is self cleansing, during your period.

We should all thank God Almighty for this, privilege for us women. Plus, Take care women.

However, the restrictive movement and slowing down, of the flow of you r period, could be as a result of SOME but NOt ALL aNTispychotics, so make sure you're on the right one.

<u>(Ps), THERE</u> are probably oral tablets to temporarily stop the flow of a period, when the DR is carrying out medical examination, I don't know.

<u>FURTHERMORE,</u> **Please Note that, <u>anti-psychotics medication, taken in broad day light, can be dangerous if abused.</u>**

If given for a prolonged period of time, it becomes a sedative drug. When it puts you to sleep. The danger of this is:-

1. if exposed to the surrounding of the wrong people, you could be abducted,
2. you could be harmed in the sleep, or incapacitated.
3. If there is a fire, you may burn with it.

<u>Again, anti-psychotics medication, can be dangerous if abused.</u> When increased, could prevent the muscles in your hands, from not working properly, may give **tremors,** then instead of being able to fuck yourself through masturbation, **it may lead to sexual captivity in that you may become promiscuous, consequently.**

The flipping psychiatrist, lures you to sleep with a man you are not in love with, to be getting pregnant for him as well. If you refuse to comply, **it may lead to further sexual captivity in that you may become promiscuous, consequently,** you may catch disease.

Stimulating an individual, to charge him or her up with Viagra, or Aphrodisiac, in order for victim _to level up sexually to those that have become, loose females as well males,_ should, should be punishable. You're going to need deliverance, if you are a Christian O!

Why should other peoples', sexual problems', be your problem!

Which I pray it, deliverance also works, as if the pastor doesn't know/ or if he knows, but doesn't say what is wrong with you. Then you are at the mercy of those giving you a sexual stimulant, after <u>if</u> being sedated with <u>antipsychotic</u> drugs <u>GIVEn IN BROAD DAY LIGHT,</u> <u>that is</u> so called meant to heal your metal health illness O <u>Or if the antipsychotic is administered with the intention to harm.</u>

Those in authority say they are protecting people. But yet, vulnerable people get lied to about their 'vulnerability. How can that individual defend his or herself against maltreatment. Or how can the individual manage their vulnerability better, if it is concealed. Tell me, if God doesn't need you here anymore, that is what he should say, you don't need cancer, or any terminal illness, to die from.

But we all know the truth that cancer kills.

People want the truth not lies.

Who are you, who is responsible for your difficulties in life? Also, I don't think it is right that the government should force women with *Mental health* issues, to take contraceptive not to have children if they want to have children. In the first instance, if a Christian Pastor, tells a woman, God doesn't want her to have children, then it is the woman's choice to accept this or not. But the Authorities in that country she lives in, has no right to force their contraceptives on her *do they know what those form of contraceptives can do damage to the female body if administered unnecessarily?*

she needs to find what works. Forcing it on her is the abuse of their authority.

First and foremost, who are we in Christ, a lot of us walk around in life not knowing who we are, not knowing our worth, so then we take whatever life throws at us. Some even go as far as committing suicide, why, because nothing they do works, their boyfriend keeps using them and dumping them, some after two weeks of dating without having sex with the men, the men leaves them, mind you no sex before marriage is your goal, some their marriage broke down, because their husband is not fulfilling their needs, he won't look after them and their child, he doesn't seem to care. Some people they are an opportunist, if they get the chance to take your life, they would do it.

We need to stop for a minute; and look at what God thinks about us and what God has to say about it all. I think we need to start by being born again, we cannot have the greatest comforter in our lives without this, and this is the Holy Ghost / Holy Spirit. He is the comforter of peace, when everything around us is falling, no friends to be found, no family just you and your boyfriend or your fiancé or just you and your husband, then believe me it is the work of the holy spirit that comforts, in that he the spirit of truth will give you an understanding of the word of God and will remind you the words of God that are in the bible, that will comfort you when you are feeling down. This is the power of the salvation of God.

KJV (King James Version) bible.

Hosea 4:6"My people are destroyed for lack of knowledge: because thou hast rejected knowledge, I will also reject thee, that thou shalt be no priest to me: seeing thou hast forgotten the law of thy God, I will also forget thy children." This simply states that we need the God of Jesus Christ in our lives.

(John 3:6-8) 6 *"That which is born of the flesh is flesh; and that which is born of the Spirit is spirit."*

7 *"Marvel not that I said unto thee, Ye must be born again."*

8 *"The wind bloweth where it listeth, and thou hearest the sound thereof, but canst not tell whence it cometh, and whither it goeth: so is every one that is born of the Spirit."*

(John14:6 -7)6"Jesus saith unto him, I am the way, the truth, and the life: no man cometh unto the Father, but by me.7 "If ye had known me, ye should have known my Father also: and from henceforth ye know him, and have seen him."

John 14:1-4

1"Let not your heart be troubled: ye believe in God, believe also in me.2 "In my Father's house are many mansions: if it were not so, I would have told you. I go to prepare a place for you." 3 "And if I go and prepare a place for you, I will come again, and receive you unto myself; that where I am, there ye may be also. 4 "And whither I go ye know, and the way ye know."

John14: 15- 31

15 "If ye love me, keep my commandments."

16 "And I will pray the Father, and he shall give you another Comforter, that he may abide with you for ever;"

17 "Even the Spirit of truth; whom the world cannot receive, because it seeth him not, neither knoweth him: but ye know him; for he dwelleth with you, and shall be in you."

18 "I will not leave you comfortless: I will come to you."

19 "Yet a little while, and the world seeth me no more; but ye see me: because I live, ye shall live also."

20 "At that day ye shall know that I am in my Father, and ye in me, and I in you."

21 "He that hath my commandments, and keepeth them, he it is that loveth me: and he that loveth me shall be loved of my Father, and I will love him, and will manifest myself to him."

22 "Judas saith unto him, not Iscariot, Lord, how is it that thou wilt manifest thyself unto us, and not unto the world?"

23 "Jesus answered and said unto him, If a man love me, he will keep my words: and my Father will love him, and we will come unto him, and make our abode with him."

24 "He that loveth me not keepeth not my sayings: and the word which ye hear is not mine, but the Father's which sent me."

John14: 25- 31

25 "These things have I spoken unto you, being yet present with you."

26 "But the Comforter, which is the Holy Ghost, whom the Father will send in my name, he shall teach you all things, and bring all things to your remembrance, whatsoever I have said unto you."

<u>*27 "Peace I leave with you, my peace I give unto you : not as the world giveth, give I unto you. Let not your heart be troubled, neither let it be afraid."*</u>

28 "Ye have heard how I said unto you, I go away, and come again unto you. If ye loved me, ye would rejoice, because I said, I go unto the Father: for my Father is greater than I."

29 "And now I have told you before it come to pass, that, when it is come to pass, ye might believe."

30 "Hereafter I will not talk much with you: for the prince of this world cometh, and hath nothing in me."

31 "But that the world may know that I love the Father; and as the Father gave me commandment, even so I do. Arise, let us go hence."

John14: 15 "If ye love me, keep my commandments." Mat 19:16-22

- Thou shalt not Kill,
- Thou shalt not commit adultery
- thou shalt not steal,
- thou shall not covet thy neighbour's house, thou shalt not covet thy neighbour's wife, nor his manservant, nor his maidservant, nor his ox, nor his ass, nor any thing that is thy neighbour's.

Are four of the Ten Commandments that are relevant to what I'm talking about in this book, which the bible says we should not do.

Mat 19:16-22

> o   16 "And, behold, one came and said unto him, Good Master, what good thing shall I do, that I may have eternal life?"
>
> o   17 "And he said unto him, why callest thou me good? there is none good but one, that is, God: but if thou wilt enter into life, keep the commandments."
>
> o   18 "He siath unto him, Which? Jesus said, Thou shalt do no murder, Thou shalt not commit adultery, Thou shalt not steal, Thou shall not bear false witness,
>
> o   19 "Honour thy father and thy mother, and Thou shalt love thy neighbor as thyself."
>
> o   20 "The young man saith unto him, All these things have I kept from my youth up: what lack I yet?"
>
> o   21 *Jesus said unto him, If thou will be perfect, go and sell that thou hast, and give to the poor, and thou shalt have treasure in heaven: and come and follow me.*"
>
> o   22 "But when the young man heard that saying, he went away sorrowful: for he had great possessions."

What the above scripture means to me, is a lot of things, as it covers a lot of things. But going straight to the main point or if you like the significant point, is that when God wants us to serve him, he will call, so then when we hear the call, we should then serve him.

This doesn't mean you cannot have a job you go to, if you are not in Full time ministry.

Also, if you don't understand anything, about this scripture, them please ask the man/woman of God. But if you are not a Christian, then you need to go f ind a church Pastor who can explain this scripture to you better.

I believe if a woman is in a relationship where she feels the neglect her man is giving her can kill her, then she needs to move on with her life.

For example, You dashed your foot against the bed and your toe nail nearly came off, he didn't warn you to be careful; and he calls himself a pastor.

I'm telling you now, that man doesn't love you. Because they have the gift of prophecy and they don't tell you nothing. Sometimes they might tell you, but If you forget then it's your fault. the point is he didn't try to warn you at all. This is neglect. The day they might lose you to cancer, so the next selfish can step in, this would be so Sad. *There are a lot of Hypocrites in the church. Just be careful and look after yourselves.*

[NIV Mat 5:28,31-32] and (NIV Mat 19:3-12) 3 "Some Pharisees came to him to test him. They asked, "Is it lawful for a man to divorce his wife for any and every reason?"

4 "Haven't you read," he replied, "that at the beginning the Creator 'made them male and female,"

5 "and said, 'For this reason a man will leave his father and mother and be united to his wife, and the two will become one f lesh'?"

6 "So they are no longer two, but one f lesh. Therefore what God has joined together, let no one separate."

7 "Why then," they asked, "did Moses command that a man give his wife a certificate of divorce and send her away?"

8 "Jesus replied, "Moses permitted you to divorce your wives because your hearts were hard. But it was not this way from the beginning."

9 "I tell you that anyone who divorces his wife, _except for sexual_ immorality, and marries another woman commits adultery."

10 "The disciples said to him, "If this is the situation between a husband and wife, it is better not to marry."

11 "Jesus replied, "Not everyone can accept this word, but only those to whom it has been given."

12 "For there are eunuchs who were born that way, and there are eunuchs who have been made eunuchs by others—and there are those who choose to live like eunuchs for the sake of the kingdom of heaven. The one who can accept this should accept it."

Mat 19:9 "I tell you that anyone who divorces his wife, except for sexual immorality, and marries another woman commits adultery."

I personally don't believe that a woman should allow herself to get fat and then she becomes miserable. Please look after your weight, so that you can look good for yourselves first then for your man. If you put on weight your man is supposed to help you lose the weight, through a weight management plan or something, not for him to put you away through divorce because of it, or to add to your weight problem, by keeping you fat so that he can continue his manipulations in your life. Whatever kind of control you might be subject to in your relationship this is not good, so seek help, in order to be free from this.

Once again, I believe if a woman is in a relationship where she feels the neglect her man is giving her can kill her/ if he/her feels that they are subject to control in their relationship, then he/her needs to move on with their life. You will not be able to progress with your life in that relationship and you will live a miserable life if you are being subject to control in this way. Basically if you are leaving the marriage for a good reason, like the man or woman neglects, then I'm not saying divorce is good, but this should be okay, after you tried to work it out and had the same problems over and over again. Think about the things that really makes you unhappy before you leave the marriage. If they are really upsetting and very serious, then the choice to leave is yours. But after the first divorce do not do divorce again good luck.

Some leave their marriage because they are subject to control in their relationship, because there is no respect for each other, no love just control. This is why we should be sure we are in love with our partners, before we say I do.

This world is certainly evil. The people who you try to help are the now, home wreckers. God will judge them. Why can't people go find their own man please, instead of other people's man.

God has given me a gift to help people and nothing in this world, no Delilah no jezebel will stop me..

what would make me stay in a good relationship, is if he spiritually neglected me and the child if any, I could live with that, as God will not give you more than you can cope, but if he met physical need help with cooking, treat the child(ren) good and kindly, be there when they are sick.

buy me and the child(ren) gifts, not be sarcastic, encourages instead of pessimism, then I would work at a marriage that has spiritual neglect. The point of it is if he doesn't show he cares then it might not work.

Though I think if you care about someone you would not play games with them and you would tell them all you want them to know through prophecies. Note, we who have accepted, our Lord Jesus Christ, are God's children, so then if he doesn't give us a dream, about how big or subordinate, he wants us to be, this doesn't mean that God is playing games with us. He loves us, and he knows why he reveals things to us when he is ready. We should pray for revelations in our dreams. Or from his good faithful servants, leaders of the church, to us, however he wants to speak to us or move in our lives. *Either way, God can speak through my husband, or a man of God or anyone else, or preferably God can talk directly to me through my dreams, no matter how big or how subordinate God wants me to be, at least this would be crystal clear, you would not lie to the person, there would be no secrets between you he has to accept the way God has made you.*

But I tell you this any man who doesn't prophesy into his wife's life, by protecting her from harm, but is being all lovey dovey, is only a deceiver and doesn't love you. The day you will die because of their neglect, God will judge them. But I also realise that no one can protect you all the time, so you have to look after yourself.

KJV Rev 21:7-8 "He that overcometh shall inherit all things; and I will be his God, and he shall be my son."

8 "But the fearful and unbelieving, and the abominable, and murderers, and whoremongers, and sorcerers, and idolaters, and all liars, shall have their part in the lake which burneth with fire and brimstone: which is the second death."

The rev21:8 simply means, because some are afraid of the future, they go to the extent of murdering people, deceiving and cheating people, the rest is self explanatory.

KJV I Corinthians 14 :1-2 "Follow after charity, desire spiritual gifts, but rather that ye prophecy"

2 "For he that speaketh in an unknown tongue speaketh not unto men, but unto God: for no man understandeth him; howbeit in the spirit he speaketh mysteries."

<u>Romans 10 :11 "For the scripture saith, whosoever believeth on him shall not be ashamed."</u>

<u>Joel 2 :27-29, "And ye shall know that I am in the midst of Isreal, and that I am the LORD your God, and none else : and my people shall never be ashamed."</u>

28 "And it shall come to pass afterwards, that I will pour out my spirit upon all f lesh; and your sons and your daughters shall prophecy, your old men shall dream dreams, your young men shall see visions:"

29 "And also upon the servants and upon the handmaidens in those days will I pour out my spirit.

Act 2:17 "And it shall come to pass in the last days, saith the God, I will pour out of my spirit upon all f lesh: and your sons and daughters shall prophecy, and your young men shall see visions, and your old men shall dream dreams."

18 "And on my servants and on my handmaidens I will pour out in those days of my spirit; and they shall prophecy:"

Heb5:14, "But strong meat belongeth to them that are of full age, even those who by reason of use have their senses exercised to discern both good and evil."

James1:5 "If any of you lack wisdom, let him ask of God, that giveth to all men liberally, and upbraideth not; and it shall be given him."

1 Peter 4:8 & James 5:20 "Let him know that he which covereth the sinner from the error of his way shall save a soul from death, and shall hide a multitude of sins."

I John 1:9-10 "If we confess our sins, he is faithful and just to forgive us our sins, and to cleanse us from all unrighteousness."

10 [If we say we have not sinned, we make him a liar and his word is not in us].

In a nut shell these scriptures are God's thoughts about lies, deceit, and that if we repent of our sins by confessing them to God he is faithful and just to forgive us our sins. If you want to you can confess to a pastor but this is optional. The important thing is that you repent of your sins through confession to him God in prayer and stop it. Also, that it is possible for someone to see in their dream if God wants them to serve as a Nanny or as a Nurse etc, then this is the prophecy, yes, it is ! This is emphasised in the quote, Acts 2:18 "And on my servants and on my handmaidens I will pour out in those days of my spirit: and they shall prophecy:"

Notwithstanding, if dreams like prophecies don't happen to you, then maybe a man of God who you know to be faithful in your life will hear from God for you. You will know it's true, when you know your capacity.

Another point is that, if a married man proposes to a single lady by deception that he is not married; and God didn't show her in a dream that he is a married man.

But then she finds out after their marriage, that he is a married man, this shows that she is a vulnerable lady. Also, she can choose to leave him if she wants to, or choose not to leave him as another man might lie to her in the same way again. And any man who deceives a woman in this way will get the judgment of God.

However, polygamy without the consent of the woman, should be against the law plus should be illegal, also any man, lying about his marital status should be illegal, meaning, irrespective of her vulnerability or the silly lesson the man wants to teach her, if a married man doesn't tell a singlet single lady the truth about his marital status immediately, lying about his marital status should be illegal, as a married man should get the consent of the single woman, about if she wants to continue with the married man. Though I don't know, what female will want to go on with this. Nevertheless, it's a matter of personal choice.

He has a responsibility to tell the single lady, his girlfriend the truth about his marital status immediately. As if this is not legalised, then the government is slack in their duty to protect vulnerable adults from conduits. Polygamy is only wrong and is only an abuse for a woman, if it's against the consent of my God of Jesus Christ; and the male in question, has to get the consent of the female in question as well.

People who choose polygamy, it is then their choice, but I definitely think that, if a married man is allowed to have a girlfriend, _then he should be obligated_, to tell her his marital status immediately. If caught lying and wasting her time, should be given a lenient fine./charge.

Hence, no man should be allowed to play games such as guessy guessy 7, 6, or 9 with the singlet, that is not on at all.

I would hope that she would maintain her virtues O under all circumstances. If deceived by a married man about his marital status, by the time it's the moment of truth; the bottom line is that she would have known before hand, that, we only know who we love, but we don't know who loves us back; and that in this case, she had been dating a married man; and she didn't know all this while, as God didn't reveal it to her. I would hope that she kept her virtues O.

Remember whether it is the case that a married man has a girlfriend, or a man has two wives, it is the same thing that is going on here.

But why would God want this I don't know. I know it is easier said than done when you are under the influence of Viagra / aphrodisiac, instead of controllable natural sexual urges. But you just have to try to be holy and do your best.

It is just like being under the influence of psychiatric drugs, it's just a battle that is tough. Because it will become harder to fast when you are given psychiatric medication, but again you just have to try. Again, why evil people like to disturb people who are minding their own business, I do not know.

You become fat on their drugs, you may or may not get diagnosed with something, then to become a sex tool, is but to name a few of what anti- psychotic medication can do to you. When it is prolonged for longer than necessary, then it turns from a supportive medication, to an abusive drug that I believe it is no longer a medication to make you well, for when you are either, (depressed, stressed etc. etc.).

This is why we need God to intervene if he will.

I think after your depression, the drugs are supposed to be stopped, but instead the psychiatrist keep forcing you to stay on it like you are some sort of criminal, who is in prison.

They could just pick on you ; randomly section you if you are noncompliant. Who the hell are all these people? If they got something to say about taking you out of this world then they should be a man about it and come to the open about it. They are dishonest people, in Uniform; and I have no respect for people <u>who molest people</u> and eventually kills them with their drugs in broad day light without their knowledge. <u>I'm not saying the authorities will kill you definitely, but just to be aware</u> of the possibility of manipulation.

What seems to be the problem ? If God don't need you alive anymore, then maybe he should come to your face about it, because as it stands, why would you want to leave a vulnerable under 20 years old child, alone with strangers in this strange world. It makes no sense to me at all, this is cruelty.

If they know they wanted to get rid of you, then my question is, why did they let you bring an innocent life into the world, who cannot defend for themselves?

I also feel that, you do not need a vulnerability to show that you need help from God, the question now is, why are you vulnerable, to the point that it could lead to early termination? Because if God really don't want you to be alive anymore, why not tell you to your face, because it's like people in authority are playing games with you, when they don't tell you what is wrong with you.

Anyway, I don't understand this and I don't get it. Bu I'll keep believing and trusting in God until death parts me from this world.

Furthermore, I reinforce that, despite all embarrassments, temptation and all that, I want you to be aware of something, I used to get angry at God for my mishaps /mistakes made in life, bad decisions, though I am now not angry at God for the temptations I face, neither am I saying God is bad, but I am just trying to make a way of escape if you like out of a difficult situation. Also, trying to make a way to manage temptations as a believer or as an infidel- a non believer of Christ. Remember God is sovereign, and he makes things perfect in his own time.

I will bless the God who gives and takes away. I have many reasons to be thankful to God.

1. *He blessed me with an amazing child,*
2. *he wakes me up to see a good day every day,*
3. *He gives me hope for tomorrow*
4. *He has sustained me up until now*
5. *He is my inspiration*
6. *He makes me happy and not sad*
7. *He helps me to overcome my challenges*
8. *He is my Rock*
9. *He is my friend*
10. *Above all, he is good and his Mercies endureth forever.*

Also, I'd like to say this, in my own personal opinion, I feel that some witch Drs are reasonable people, meaning that they do what they feel is right for them. I believe that everyone has a freedom of right to express what they believe in, <u>as long as it has nothing to do with harming, others nor me personally or don't try their magic on me.</u>

I may not believe in what they practice, but it is their right *<u>to practice it in some countries.</u>*

However, I want you to note that, I don't believe all witch Drs practice voodoo. But the ones, <u>alongside ordinary people,</u> who do practice voodoo, are harmful and can destroy people's lives. To be honest, I never want to have anything to do with these kind of people, or have any form of contact with such people in my life.

<u>*My question would be, why does God want to force you to do Polygamy, if you are not interested in that? But only if the clergy may be lying that God said this to him /her to tell you to do polygamy that is. You may try it, if it works out then it's of God if it doesn't then it's not of God, because God never lies.*</u>

<u>*If you really don't trust what the clergy is saying to you about Polygamy, then don't do it, refrain from it if you can.*</u>

<u>*As I remember it, when God created man, he gave the man free will, I put before you Life and death, choose life that you may live.*</u>

God only advises he doesn't force, therefore any sexual urge that is not natural from when two people who love each other touch each other, but if stimulated by aphrodisiac or Viagra, that makes you desperate to share a man with another woman in a Polygamous home, is aphrodisiac or Viagra, a sexual drug, or potion, which then becomes Witchcraft and manipulation in the church!

<u>*Polygamy could lead to your termination, if the man is pretending to love you, he might get rid of you, because he has another favorite wife, so think before accepting polygamy, then if you do, think if you want to bring children into that relationship, only if the man doesn't truly love you back. But highly unlikely that it could lead to your termination, just to*</u> be cautious if the man truly loves you or not! *Even in a monogomous relationship, <u>if a man doesn't love you and knows you are vulnerable,</u>* he could take advantage of you, it could lead to him using and dumping you, so the next selfish can step in.

<u>On the other hand, Polygamy has it's uses, only if it is instructed by God that this is what you should do because of your vulnerability, even then you shouldn't be pressured to go into it because of sexual</u>

urges, only if you agree with God to do it, as God said, "I put before you life and death, choose life that you might live," so no man should coerse you, cajole or force you into polygamy or even a monogomous relationship it should be your chioce only.

But if I were to choose, I'd choose a monogomous relationship that I can trust and then hope and pray nothing bad will happen to me, despite my vulnerability. Because if I don't get the man I love, then I'd rather stay by myself then.

Note the following applies to if you want polygamy,

- It is a marriage with a married man who has a wife:

  - You may have children if you trust that the man loves you, and please try to trust him!
  - It may last, or worst case scenario leead to your termination, but highly unlikely, just to be cautious if the man truly loves you or not!
  - It stops you sleeping around hence prevents sexually transmitted disease
  - The truth is known early that he is married
  - It's because God said you should do it, not sexual urges
  - You consent to it and are in agreement with God about this request for your life.

Note the following applies to if you want monogamous relationship:

- It is a relationship between one male and one female.
- It stops you sleeping around hence prevents sexually transmitted disease
- The guy might hide his girlfriend use and dump you, when he gets all he wants so his true lover can step in, he may dump you.
- I prefer monogomous irrespective and will carefully choose a monogomous partner....................

.................If you are vulnerable and don't want to be molested by a dishonest, untrustworthy, unscrupulous so called friend you let do sleep over in your home, as a deep sleeper because it could happen, if you decide not to take either monogamous or polygamous relationship, where the man can be your protector, then, maybe your family should _care_ about you; and keep you close to them so they can make sure that you are safely protected by them instead, until you find a Mr right then. God bless.

I repeat reiterate that, if you are vulnerable and don't want to be molested by a dishonest, untrustworthy, unscrupulous so called friend you let do sleep over in your home, as a deep sleeper because it could happen. _Because the relevant bad friend (s) who can possibly get someone to sexually assault you meaning rape you in the sleep, so be careful. How did the witch Dr whom the authorities back up, get into your property, probably through a bad friend, or the private landlord has spare keys to your flat._

I think an uncaring family would push you out to expose you to this form of danger, because they are jealous and don't wish you well. Also, they're the type of INCONSIDERATE family that, will be controlling as well nagging, so you can run away from them.

What did God tell them to tell you, because they are not oblige to inform you the truth, though they may not harm you personally, but might push you to those who might or might not harm you !

But I'd advice that you stay clear of contraceptives as I've explained somewhere in this book, contraceptives are evil, I think in page range _12- 24_ about sterilisation etc. etcetera. I believe contraceptives might be used only if there is a critical medical condition for a female, so stay clear off them please they can be evil if administered, given perhaps for the wrong reason.

Pay attention to your dreams, if God reveals to you in your dream to be careful around some or a member of your family, then becareful then. Even if you have to go live away from them for a while then so be it, till when God says return because this could happen if your family is being negligent, because if they were being honest in the first place, you wouldn't need to escape from their harassments. Good luck and God bless. A family who doesn't control, but wishes the best for you, is who you should be around. By their good advise that has been working *for years* or months, for you is how you'll know they love you.

KJV Prov 24 : 6 *"For by wise counsel thou shalt make thy war: and in multitude of counsellors there is safety."*

KJV Prov 15 :22 *"Without counsel purposes are disappointed: but in the multitude of counsellors they are established."*

Also, in all circumstances, don't get it twisted, Polyg A My *is not for the purpose so you can turn into a child minder. If you want to be a child minder, then be one by yourself and get paid,* not because you need sex in a polygamous relationship.

cccc*Also. I am not saying if you do agree to do Polygamy, that you can not offer to babysit for the other female counterpart as well, likewise she can help you out too, ……*

………but not for you to be lured into polygamy through sexual urges to fufill all what the couples want, if God didn't say it is what he wants you to do, also that you agree with God, as God doesn't force, he said, "I place before you life and death, choose life that you might live," so therefore make your choice. Remember if you want to vulunteer fine, and if you want that childminder job to be your occupation fine too. But keep your sex life pure, holy and under control. Thank you & God bless.

Otherwise, get yourself a job you like and let God bless you, God bless.

If a man of God hears from God and he is not 419 pastor a liar, then he would tell you what instructions God has to say about Polygamy and you. Shalom !!!

On the other hand, one of the influences of the witch Dr as well people in authority, is to control an individual's person's life. One of the tools they use, may be derived from aphrodisiac /Viagra a love potion, or medicine. Which can lead to the following if care is not take:-

1. *it can lead to promiscuity,*
2. *prostitution,*
3. *possibly disease for both male or female, which we all know, disease is deadly,*
4. *cervical cancer for the woman, which we all know cancer kills, then eventually death,*

KJV Romans 6 :23 "For the wages of sin is death ; but the gift of God is eternal life through Jesus Christ our Lord."

Polygamy is the same thing as a married man having a girlfriend, so both can be legalised for consenting adults.

Polygamy is only wrong and is only an abuse for a woman, if it's against the consent of my God of Jesus Christ; and the male in question, has to get the consent of the female in question as well.

So then, if the man doesn't tell her the truth about his marital status <u>IMMEDIATELY,</u> then does he have intentions to harm the singlet lady? So then if caught, he should be punished accordingly. Also, if he wants two wives then hat is what he should do. As a man who has a wife and a girlfriend, they have this silly attitude and habit, that they can manipulate her and abuse her in the way they cannot treat their <u>iMPORTANT,</u> wife that they put in the house. I am talking from what I have witnessed.

I for one is a big fan of a monogamous relationship, meaning being in a one to one relationship, with my husband my man whatever you want to call him, to myself alone.

If you've got a lot going from you, you don't have to take this, like if you are intelligent, then you know that already, then you have a lot going for you; then trust in God, that he is able to bring your own man to you, hence you might not need to do Polygamy, unless God has instructed the man of God that is what you should be doing, then if there is a weakness in your life, you can see if it is true then, when the man of God proves this weakness that is in your life.

Also just because you have been told by the man of God, that /God has instructed him to tell you to do Polygamy, <u>DOESN'T MEAN YOU CANNOT BE OPEN TO HAVING CHILDREN, IN A POLYGAMOUS HOME, THE CHOICE TO HAVE OR NOT HAVE CHILDREN IS YOURS;</u> and it doesn't mean that God wants you to be doing the thinking of the other wife for her, by sharing with her your gifts and talents.

But I'd advise that there is no need for hostility, try to help each other as women, and try not to fight or have misunderstandings but if she is rude to you, you might switch from giving the other wife any little or big help that you share with her, it's just a natural instinct, so Good luck.

Plus be open minded to the situation surrounding Polygamy, be open to the fact that it is okay to still have children, even in a polygamous home.

Nevertheless, I just feel that, every woman should have the opportunity to get their own man who will take the responsibility to look after her and the children, if they have any.

Polygamy is only wrong and is only an abuse for a woman, if it's against the consent of my God of Jesus Christ; and the male in question, has to get the consent of the female in question as well.

I hereby ask, when should the wisdom of men, which God gives to all men liberally, when they ask be used to start polygamy for a vulnerable woman? James 1:5 King James Version (KJV)

5 "If any of you lack wisdom, let him ask of God, that giveth to all men liberally, and upbraideth not; and it shall be given him."

However if it is accepted by God, then it is also wrong and is an abuse for a woman, if it is done secretly without the knowledge of all consenting parties. So why lie when God is not a liar.

I am not saying polygamy is wrong, as no man of God has ever told me that polygamy is wrong, but I don't believe in a man marrying two wives as IF YOU are NOT under the inf luence of Viagra or aphrodisiac, THEN WHY DO YOU NEED SEX then? But at the end of the day it is up to you.

Let us say for instance a man/woman of God and it should only be a man/woman of God that tells you this, that "God wants you to do polygamy because of the weakness(es) in your life which makes you vulnerable to, possibly subject to abuse, control, manipulation, *or being harmed by a secret enemy of yours,* or an evil person." Before you take polygamy, remember that Polygamy in itself can be controlling, and that it is probably the inf luence of a sexual drug that led you to it. You are being controlled by the police and those medics in authority.

Try not to get angry because you feel that those in authority are trying to control your sex drive with a sexual drug, with the intention to ruin your life, because I know it is easier said than done, but if you lose your self-control ; and hit someone, it could lead to you being prosecuted or sectioned in a Psychiatric ward, them you have helped them to easily achieve their aim.

This is torture and hell on earth, I know, but just try.

However, please when they "to whom it may concern," openly <u>shows</u> you your weakness which is the reason why they said God said you need to do Polygamy marriage in the first place; and you must get this proof. When you are satisfied with the decision, *if you want you may* get a good contraceptive so that you don't get pregnant if you have no child. *Or you may be open to having children if you take polygamy, the choice is yours, do what's best for you.*

If when your weaknesses are brought to light, it is still down to you to decide if you want to take polygamy, even if God advices you to take it, God will not force you unless it is important. I repeat and reiterate that, ….

<u>…………If you are vulnerable and don't want to be molested as a deep sleeper because it could happen, if you decide not to take either monogomous or polygamous relationship, where the man can be your protector, then, maybe your family should care about you; and keep you close to them so they can make sure that you are safely protected by them instead, *until you find a mr right then.* God bless.</u>

But I'd advice that you stay clear of contraceptives as I've explained somewhere in this book, contraceptives are evil, I think in page range <u>12-22</u> about sterilisation etc. etcetera. I believe contraceptives might be used only if there is a critical medical condition for a female, so stay clear off them please they can be evil if administered, given perhaps for the wrong reason.

Or use condom during love making, if you like condom, some people don't like condom, for a reason, I didn't wish to go into as it's personal, but I'll tell you the reason in a minute. But if you have one child already, then have no more than three or less than < three. *Also don't think you are the first lady of the house, as his important wife, is the first lady. Why you need sex for when you don't have a man to yourself, I don't know? But I don't think polygamy is a sin, but neither do I like it, nor do I think it is necessary ! Let me know if I am wrong about that Polygamy is not necessary !!!*

Basically, *don't use rubber with any man you don't trust, as they might go too fast and the rubber might go deep in you. Also, condom can split at the side, so be careful you have been warned.*

Your man is supposed to take care of you remember that, and I don't know about you, but I don't like a man who is always shouting at me for no reason.

Still love God please I mean this, I'm not being sarcastic either, you don't want to upset God and then he might send you to hell.

Hypothetically speaking, let's say you are from the Philippines and you are British, I wouldn't go to my home country to get a guy, as they might use you for papers, unless of course you really want to go to your home country to get someone to marry. I would try to find someone in the UK; and if the men in the UK cannot be trusted with your vulnerability if you don't find one that will look after you and the potential children you will have, this is to say if you find this out, then the men are saying you are not worthy to have your own family.

But if you feel actually going to get someone from your home country is better, then please do what is in your best interest. This is only an advise.

I would either listen to the pastor in the UK, that God wants me to do polygamy in the UK because of your vulnerability *as a deep sleeper,* which they will show you clearly; that possibly you're subject to abuse, control, manipulation, or being harmed, by a secret enemy of yours, or an evil person."

My question would be, why does God want to force you to do Polygamy, if you are not interested in that? But only if the clergy may be lying that God said this to him /her to tell you to do polygamy that is. You may try it, if it works out then it's of God if it doesn't then it's not of God, because God never lies.

If you really don't trust what the clerg y is saying to you about Polygamy, then don't do it, refrain from it if you can.

As I remember it, when God created man, he gave the man free will, I put before you Life and death, choose life that you may live.

God only advises he doesn't force, therefore any sexual urge that makes you desperate to share a man with another woman in a Polygamous home, is aphrodisiac or Viagra, a sexual drug, or potion, which then becomes Witchcraft and manipulation in the church!

On the other hand, one of the inf luences of the witch Dr as well people in authority, is to control an individual's person's life. One of the tools they use, may be derived from aphrodisiac /Viagra a love potion, or medicine. Which can lead to the following if care is not take:-

1. *it can lead to promiscuity,*
2. *prostitution,*
3. *possibly disease for both male or female, which we all know, disease is deadly,*
4. *cervical cancer for the woman, which we all know cancer kills, then eventually death,*

KJV Romans 6 :23 "For the wages of sin is death ; but the gift of <u>God is eternal life</u>

kJV Prov 24 : 6 "For by wise counsel thou shalt make thy war: and in multitude of counsellors there is safety."

KJV Prov 15:22 "Without counsel purposes are disappointed: but in the multitude of counsellors they are established."

You have to tell them to prove that you are vulnerable, if they don't, I would refuse polygamy, as if you have weakness(es) and they don't tell you, then they are trying to control you, through making you think that you are safe, when actually you are not. Polygamy therefore might terminate you. So then look for your own man.

However, I think it's highly unlikely that polygamy might terminate you, you need to think if you like it or not, or if you want to stay by yourself, if you cannot find a man to yourself then.

John 8:32 "Then you will know the truth, and the truth will set you free."

John 8:32 This is to say, that the information you are told about yourself/weakness(es) will help you make a better informed decision about what to do with your life. So then, anything less< than this, is a lie from the pit of hell, hence you may be abused, controlled, or put to harm. You are hereby, living a lie, or in denial unknowingly, as you will need to face up to the facts of your hopefully temporary situation to soon be, crystal clear.

As it stands, if you look well and are well, and nothing is wrong with you, I would believe in myself, that I am who God says I am, I am what I am by the Grace of God. As when your mum gave birth to you, there was nothing wrong with you, you were not a disabled, you are whole in The Lord Jesus's name, if you are intelligent, then you know that already, then you have a lot going for you; then trust in God, that he is able to bring your own man to you. Only if those asking you to do polygamy, says you have weaknesses, but they don't prove it, then believe nothing is wrong with you, if all the previous things I mentioned are true in your life.

Also even when they prove your weakness, believe it is temporary and that there is nothing too difficult for God to change, but please either then take polygamy if they instruct by God/ wisdom, in the previously explained way, or stay by yourself if you wish, if you don't believe in it all.

Notwithstanding, if Polygamy is at the decision of the divine, intervention of The supernatural God of my Lord Jesus Christ/ the instruction through the wisdom of men. So anything that God has not instructed I don't want to do it, and no matter how much God tells you to do Polygamy, you don't have to have a baby, if you are worried about their safety, because of being the one, whom God has instructed/ the wisdom of men has instructed you to do polygamy, due to weakness, that may cause others to Abuse/Harm you.

As the last thing, a woman who has weakness in her life, that because of this is subject to polygamy, brings child(ren) into polygamous home, then, the children are used to do experiments. I strongly believe that if you are with a man in a polygamous relationship, who knows God, then the children will be safe, and they will not be used in experiment, they will be well cared for. Do not be afraid for if God be with you, who can be against you and your children. _Also how you will know God is with you is as I have been explaining throughout this book, is through good prophecies that have been real in your life._

And do not do Polygamy marriage for a stupid reason like all the men are taken, this is the lie from the pit of hell, if nothing is wrong with you, you can get a man to yourself. Common sense should tell you that it is a con in this case.

When the one mama met the one papa they have children that will be the next Nannies, Doctors, Lawyers etc. Not when two mama's met a Papa. Not to use vulnerable ladies to do a linage of nannies through the reason of Polygamy. Basically, if a lady/woman, doesn't want a baby in a Polygamous home, then she shouldn't be forced, simple.

No one has the right to turn anyone into a Nanny without the consent of the person involved, or without the consent of a Godly intervention, everyone should be entitled to an education, this is not the slavery days.

Before you study, maybe you should really hear from God, because I felt like I heard from God, that was why I went to study where I did. But as a matter of fact he was trying to get my attention after my studies, so I forgot some of the design skills I was taught eventually, though I must admit, they were quite basic.

I just want to say, that sometimes, we may feel ready to study a particular course, like tailoring, but your course leader advices that you do design instead, and that you can come back to tailoring later, as designing incorporates some tailoring and pattern cutting skills. I would say think about it, and try to come to a decision, as they are professionals, they usually advice sincerely, and not with intentions, to stop you progressing to your potential. Sometimes it could be the case that that it is God trying to get your attention.

I would hope that the tutors, will teach properly and not withhold the knowledge from you.

Therefore, it should be illegal for tutors to be wasting students time in the classroom, and not to teach them properly.

Because sometimes we are ready to learn, but when we graduate, God want's our attention, because he want's to show that he is with us, then you f ind that after you graduate, you get a psychiatric condition, such as stress, paranoia, depression and the likes of these, which some psychiatric specialist could take to the extreme if care is not taken. Then you forget all you learn anyway if you didn't get someone to mentor you on how to continue your design skills, alongside managing a mental health condition, that could get you killed if the medication administered is given in an abusive manner, as some are given at a high dosage and could have detrimental side effects. But only if the psychiatric knows what he/she is doing you will not have a bad experience.

I personally, don't think that teachers should limit the knowledge of students as they are there to teach. So that the pupils can graduate with the necessary skills needed in order to make it in life. It is wrong to limit students knowledge, as everyone deserves the chance to make it in life, and deserves the opportunity to be able to provide for themselves.

Education tests your ability and capacity to understand a course. Hence this is why there are different levels to prove your level of capacity and knowledge.

I believe everyone should be educated to A 'levels standard *at least before being told that God wants them to become a nanny* and if possible Be able to do beyond this, a Degree if not told that they are asked by God to become a nanny. Also, all nannies should have the intermediate knowledge of how to use Ms office application, and even people who are considered as labourers rather than called professionals. A lso in every family where someone is called by God to become nann(ies), here maybe 1 or two or more professionals there. This is the joy of family life, that we are not all called to serve.

Also, just because you are a nanny, doesn't mean you should *deliberately sleep off at night, is this lazy ? If you are able to stay up for an hour then do so, you're not on medication are you*? You need to try to discipline yourself; try to be doing night vigil at midnight from

11pm/23:00pm upwards to pray for an hour. It's up to you, you don't have to do this, even if it's that you stay up for an hour to pray it's okay if you do like to do this.

On the other hand, if they can prove to you your weakness(es), then you can choose polygamy if you wish, or not to. It would have been good if God can show you a dream about this request, and about how great, or subordinate, he wants you to be.

I repeat for the last time, PLEASE NOTE, that, in this book, I will mention the word vulnerable a lot. I AM NOT SAYING YOU ARE VULNER ABLE BECAUSE YOU ARE A FEMALE, NO I'M NOT SAYING THIS, but simply saying that, one of the things that makes you vulnerable amongst other issues, is if you are a deep sleeper.

Take a sleep test, let someone you trust anyone that you trust, draw on your arm with a washable biro a star or scorpion if you don't wake up soon, this will soon show you that you are a deep sleeper ; and people can molest you if you are around the wrong people so be careful.

Because sometimes instead of a dream, God wants us to think about what we are going into before we go into it.

Heb 5:14 *"But strong meat belongeth to them that are of full age, even those who by reason of use have their senses exercised to discern both good and evil."*

If it is confirmed that polygamy is Godly, then polygamy in itself thereby is okay, *but is not to use vulnerable ladies to do a linage of nannies job through the reason of polygamy.*

If you take polygamy, respect the man involved, don't be rude to him or his wife unless it is called for; and there is no need for hostility, help each other out, but if the other female becomes rude, or funny, then you may choose not to get involved with helping her anymore.

Also don't think you are the first lady of the house, as his <u>IMPORTA NT</u> wife, is the first lady

I want you to understand one thing, being under the influence of Viagra or aphrodisiac, could lead to unwilful sexual acts of either:

I If you are vulnerable and don't want to be molested by a dishonest, untrustworthy, unscrupulous so called friend you let do sleep over in your home, as a deep sleeper because it could happen, if you decide not to take either monogamous or polygamous relationship, where the man can be your protector, then, maybe your family should <u>care</u> about you; and keep you close to them so they can make sure that you are safely protected by them instead, until you find a Mr right then. God bless.

I want you to understand one thing, being under the influence of Viagra or aphrodisiac, could lead to unwilful sexual acts, Such as in the following:

1. ***promiscuity, Prostitution***
2. ***polygamy or***
3. ***lesbianism, gay, (Homosexuality)***

First and foremost.

I've come to the realisation, that anything is possible in this world that we are living in, because evil people are about. But we hope for the best. These are just warnings, so to guard as well prepare ourselves for the worst, before the evil penetrates into our vulnerable loved ones lives.

I'm not saying all this because it is happening, it is like if you like, a contingency plan. To be fore-warned is to be informed-!!!-!!!-6.-

First of all, RAPE is a criminal offense. Violating someone's right to consent is a criminal act. Hence, I don't think that someone would be brave enough to want to try to rape someone in the sleep, because if they get caught, they will be prosecuted by man and persecuted by the Angel of God.

But be careful, as anything is possible.

However, *You could get molested even by not the good witch, but by a bad witch DR, in the sleep, who can possibly get someone to **try to** sexually assault you meaning rape you in the sleep, so be careful. **Then, you wake up to try to get the psycho off of you. But seriously, who does this. I'll further explain.***

***How did they get into your flat, maybe a bad friend who is doing sleep over,** or perhaps the private landlord has keys to your flat, then the authorities permits the act, they are all working together o.*

(Ps), don't worry, no dishonest person, can try to rape you in the sleep, unless you let the dishonest person, into your home, even then, you'd wake up. This is why you should pick your friends carefully. So God bless.

Then the God of peace, will give you and I peace in Jesus' Name Amen.

God loves us and he wants the best for us, ...

.... God doesn't want us to be so vulnerable like a chicken, to then become a prey plus others to be the tyrant oppressors.

So, if you are vulnerable, he doesn't expect you to be molested in the sleep, he'd wake you up. Furthermore, if you're trying to molest someone, who is resting, then they'll wake up.

But note just listen to yourself, you are saying that God wants the individual to be molested.

I serve a living God, who doesn't sleep nor slumbers. (pS), THOUGH IVE NEVER SEEN HIM BEFORE IN MY LIFE.

"John 8:32 "And ye shall know the truth, and the truth shall make you free."

All the individual, needs, is the truth about the will of God for the individual's life. We don't need anymore crusades.

Even if you are physically disabled, or a vulnerable deep sleeper for now, I believe there is power in the name of Jesus, he can make even the vulnerable to be strong again.

You will get favour and help from God, God will send good people to you, who will help you. You will not be left lonely. You will get a good husband, because God only wants the best for us his children, whether, maimed, or just vulnerable or strong. Because he created us all differently.

KJV I Cor 12:25 "That there should be no schism in the body; but that the members should have the same care one for another."

As a real person, like also your ex, could be the person, spirit husband or wife, who is obsessed with you. If he or she, even a lesbian, doesn't want to let go of your relationship. He or she, even a lesbian, is the real physical man or lady, spirit husband or spirit wife, who could try to rape you in the sleep, if you are a vulnerable.

But instead of waking up immediately, but after a few seconds, you then try to get the psycho off of you. But really and truly who does that? What kind of a psycho tries to molest a vulnerable person in the sleep, for what might I ask? Note that some people, as soon as you touch them in the sleep, they wake up. They are sensitive sleepers o - !!!- !!!-6.-

Can I ask a question, would you rape a physical disabled person? This is how you know he or she, is obsessed with you; if caught he or she, will be jailed and incarcerated. Because he or she, even the lesbian partner, is jealous, twisted and evil O.

I reinforce and reiterate that, RAPE is a criminal offense, I need not remind you. Violating someone's right to consent is a criminal act. Hence, I don't think that someone would be brave enough to want to try to rape someone in the sleep, because if they get caught, they will be prosecuted by man and persecuted by the Angel of God.

But be careful, as anything is possible.

He or she if a lesbian, is only obsessed with you, because he / she wants to ruin your life, to use you first, then kill you like the devil, [he has come has come to steal to kill and to destroy, but Jesus said, he has come to give you life; and to give life more abundantly], John 10:10 KJV, that is what him and his followers do.

Psalm 116:6-8
King James Version

Ps 116:6 "The Lord preserveth the simple: I was brought low, and he helped me."

Ps 116:7 "Return unto thy rest, O my soul; for the Lord hath dealt bountifully with thee."

Ps 116:8 "<u>For thou hast delivered my soul from death, mine eyes from tears, and my feet from falling.</u>"

This is to say God will not leave you lonely-!!!-!!!6.-

In fact the bible says, let the weak say I am strong, let the poor say that I am rich.

Ecclesiastes 4:9-12
King James Version

Ecc 4:9 Two are better than one; because they have a good reward for their labour.

Ecc 4:10 For if they fall, the one will lift up his fellow: but woe to him that is alone when he falleth; for he hath not another to help him up.

Ecc 4:11 Again, if two lie together, then they have heat: but how can one be warm alone?

Ecc 4:12 And if one prevail against him, two shall withstand him; and a threefold cord is not quickly broken.

This is to say once more, God will never leave you lonely, he has a plan for the vulnerable as well the strong-!!!-!!!6.-

In fact the bible says, let the weak say I am strong, let the poor say that I am rich.

First of all,

I want to say, that no matter your vulnerability, as long as you know that God loves you, that is all that matters. So don't let anyone put you down because you have a temporary vulnerability. You are important, God has a plan for your life. You matter.

We all know no one needs a vulnerability to know the will of God for their life. Peradventure, just in case if a vulnerability is required, in order to do God's will, then surely he must know when you will be delivered.

If Housemaids are waking up at any odd times, even at midnight, totake care of their own babies.

Therefore you shouldn't need a sleep vulnerability either, nor also.

I repeat, I want you to understand one thing, being under the influence of Viagra or aphrodisiac, could lead to unwilful sexual acts.

1. **promiscuity, Prostitution**
2. **polygamy or**
3. **lesbianism, gay, (Homosexuality)**

Just to say very quickly, some people might like to say that lesbianism is a disgraceful /shameful act, but I think that, people can do whatever they want, or what they have to do, until when they're ready to realise it is wrong what they are doing,….

…to then think twice if God would be happy with what they are doing. Lastly promiscuity is something that may happen beyond someone's control, so I don't judge, then Polygamy is a choice definitely not a disgrace.

The police will tell you to take your pick indirectly when you get harassed with this sexual drug. If you get angry from the knowledge that you are being controlled in this way and you do a mistake to hit someone, who harasses you sexually, when all you want is to be with who you want or to be left alone if you cannot get who you want. They will lock you up somewhere. Sex, Lies and your soul.

If you are saying actually I don't want polygamy, I don't believe in it, and choose to stay holy by yourself like God is holy, since your spiritual weakness(es) can cause someone to *harm* you, in that you are possibly subject to abuse, control, manipulation, harm, or being made a disabled by a secret enemy of yours, or an evil person."

So then, I shouldn't need sex then may be God will take the feelings to have sex away, <u>*since he asks us, to be holy.*</u>

why then do you need sex if no man will take care of you. *Absolutely, you may be right,*…….

…….then pray to God the feeling to have sex might disappear, because sex is a sign that God wants you to be appreciated and to start a family and for intimacy. So, if you think you do not need sex, then you better pray it out of your life.

If you don't eat long enough you will die, sex is not food, if you are not worthy of a family then you don't need sex, and if you want it then get a husband *just do it with your husband and even if you think God doesn't want you to have children because of your not disability, but vulnerable condition,* then so be it. So, then you decide with your husband if having a child is the right thing for your vulnerability.

Because your children if any one of them gets the genetics of it, then they will need a good man like the father to continue them/finish them.

<u>Once again, the children if they get the genetics of it, may need to be in an organized protective, monogamous relationship that will be beneficial to both parties. If there is no guidance from your family, then be rest assured, that your family don't give a buckles about you, probably because they are jealous and don't wish you well.</u>

<u>Furthermore, vulnerable people, esp' someone who is also a vulnerable Christian, needs close guidance from a man or woman of God, a clergy, this is significantly important. They are to be Led by God at all times!!!</u>

In addition, *if you were not born as a disabled, but find that when you* grew up there are weaknesses in your life, then you are vulnerable if you are subject to abuse, or being harmed by a secret enemy of yours, or an evil person.

As I have already said earlier, if a married man proposes to a single lady by deception that he is not married; and God didn't show her in a dream that he is a married man. Then the woman has just been abused through lies.

But then she finds out after their marriage, that he is a married man, this shows that she is a vulnerable lady. Also, she can choose to leave him if she wants to, or choose not to leave him as another man might lie to her in the same way again. And any man who deceives a woman in this way will get the judgment of God.

However, polygamy without the consent of the woman, should be against the law plus should be illegal, also any man, lying about his marital status should be illegal, meaning, irrespective of her vulnerability or the silly lesson the man wants to teach her, if a married man doesn't tell a singlet single lady the truth about his marital status immediately, lying about his marital status should be illegal, as a married man should get the consent of the single woman, about if she wants to continue with the married man. Though I don't know, what female will want to go on with this. Nevertheless, it's a matter of personal choice.

He has a responsibility to tell the single lady, his girlfriend the truth about his marital status immediately. As if this is not legalised, then the government is slack in their duty to protect vulnerable adults from conduits. Polygamy is only wrong and is only an abuse for a woman, if it's against the consent of my God of Jesus Christ; and the male in question, has to get the consent of the female in question as well.

People who choose polygamy, it is then their choice, but I definitely think that, if a married man is allowed to have a girlfriend, then he should be obligated, to tell her his marital status immediately. If caught lying and wasting her time, should be given a lenient fine./charge.

However, if you find yourself in this type of Polygamous relationship through deceit, then only you can decide what to do. Ask the question, what is wrong with me that God didn't reveal to me on time this treacherous/deceptive thing. But I am now being made aware of it at this hour, by you; you meaning the man in question.

Also, if he says no reason, then he the man, is either lying and want to harm you, or there is nothing wrong with you and you have been conned/taken advantage of. However, I think stay with him if he confesses the truth to you. Try to see if you can work things out and come to an amicably or doable agreement. If you take polygamy, respect the man involved, don't be rude to him or his wife unless it is called for; and there is no need for hostility, help each other out, but if the other female becomes rude, or funny, then you may choose not to get involved with helping her anymore.

Also don't think you are the first lady of the house, as his important wife, is the first lady.

Because if you go elsewhere, things could get ugly, but if you want to risk it, then be sure to keep praying that God reveals why you were deceived in this way into the first marriage, which was a polygamous one, but whilst you look for your own man. *If you don't feel safe, stay by yourself then.*

But I think God will judge anyone who uses deceit to lure someone into a relationship that is not called for by God.

The signs that you are vulnerable are as follows;

1. *After taking a sleep test, by anyone that you trust, who may draw on your arm with a washable biro a star or scorpion if you don't wake up soon, this will soon show you that you are a deep sleeper ; and people can molest you if you are around the wrong people so be careful.*
2. *Pop belly female or male*
3. *Hair in unwanted part(s) of your body as a female*
4. *Long feet*
5. *Breast problem e.g. Cancer/no breast at all for females*
6. *Saggy breast for men*
7. *Double chin*
8. *Bald*
9. *Hair dropping out*
10. *Cancer of the womb and many more etcetera etc. etc.*

⏱ *Becoming a woman, getting Adenomyosis and Fibroid*

Moving on from my youth growing from a young girl to a lady to a woman, the transformation was when the holy spirit helped me to become a woman of age.

1 Corinthians 13 somewhere there says, [When I was a child I spoke as I a child, when I became a man, I put a way childish things]. Thanks to God, Jesus and most especially the holy spirit, who was a father as well mother figure to me. My father prayed a lot I believe that God answered his prayers.

Moving on, In June 2020, I was diagnosed with having Adenomyosis and Fibroid. This was a daunting news for me. I was asking God, why me and why this as well. But he didn't reply. I just hoped in the God of my salvation and joyed in him, and declared Lamentation 3:37 and Habakkuk 3:17

Habakkuk 3:17 NIV [New international Version] "Though the fig tree does not bud and there are no grapes on the vines, though the olive crop fails and the fields produce no food, though there are no sheep in the pen and n cattle in the stalls.

Habakkuk 3:18 "Yet I will rejoice in the Lord, I will be joyful in God my savior."

Lamentation 3:37KJVersion "Who is he that saith, and it cometh to pass, when the Lord commandeth it not?"

Habakkuk 3:17 KJV "Although the fig tree shall not blossom, neither shall fruit be in the vines, the labour of the olive shall fail, and the fields shall yield no meat, the f lock shall be cut off from the fold, and there shall be no herd in the stalls.

Habakkuk 3:18 KJV "Yet I will rejoice in the Lord, I will joy in the God of my salvation."

I still believed in a miracle working God and I am still believing in him.

Well I am exhausted, I fight every day and now I think is time to shut up and let God take control of everything disturbing my life.

I remember feeling betrayed as if the devil maliciously planted fibroid in me because someone is trying to stop me from having a baby. I went back to pray to God that he will not allow the devils children to prevail; and only his plan for my life would stand.

Rev 12:11 [We overcome by the blood of the lamb and the words of our testimony, and loved not our life to the death].

Luke 17:33 KJV "Whosoever shall seek to save his life shall lose it; and whosoever shall lose his life shall preserve it" *meaning know when to act on something and when not to act on something.*

- Mark 4:17 [Persecution arises on account of the word] be careful what you say period. Also, if persecution come don't give up. Mark 4:17 King James Version (KJV) "And have no root in themselves, and so endure but for a time; afterward, when aff liction or persecution ariseth for the word's sake, immediately they are offended."
- *In a nut shell if persecutions come, try not to be offended, so stand for what you believe in, on the other hand, if you have an opinion and you are not ready for persecution keep it to yourself then, basically think before you talk. Because some people might take offense of what you think and say, whilst some can use your words against you, be it the bible passage you believe in or your own personal words that you say.*
- *Like when you have personal plans some you can share some you cannot share, b4 (before) it surfaces, don't tell people your personal plans (e.g. & i.e. a creative idea), they can try to stop it from happening. Get yourself together first to do it first before they steal your ideas.*

Still on the topic of be careful what you say, I remember when I watched TV programs as a child, I learnt about 1 or 5 things from watching TV, no more than 5 things though.

- *Single white female, (that there are sinister people in the world)*
- *Another one was a comedy, but the message derive was to be careful not to set yourself alight over a f lame from a gas cooker if you are a young person*
- *You have the right to remain silent, keep your thoughts to yourself if you wish*
- *If someone don't appreciate you, wish them well*
- *How to express your feelings.*
- *Sunset Beach 1990's American movie (again that sinister people exist)*

Why does there have to be an EX to make you into who you are

Why does there after to be an EX to make you into who you are, what is your family there for. They leave you to wonder about. Some of the people who have made it to the top today, if their loved ones were not there to protect and guide them, they would have messed up and not gotten to the top. You cannot expect a beautiful rose tree to grow, if you allow pests to corrupt it, you are to nurture and guide and protect it from the start. Otherwise it'll be feast for pest, plain and simple.

If you are to aspire to greatness, your family would draw you closer to them wish you well and ensure no one puts aphrodisiac into your life, a love potion like Viagra to turn you on then you bang about with every Tom, Dick and Harry, then you miss your mister right. _Enforced by Christian values, always reminding, you that sex outside wedlock is wrong or not healthy._

You don't ever need to have gone into numerous sexual relationships with men to prove a F****** point, so they can prepare you for the right one. The only person you need sex with is your husband.

They cheapilise you and turn you into a cheap slaught that they think you are. We bless the God of Jesus Christ he has the power to deliver from powers of principalities and from witch doctors powers. He has been my defence and fortress, citadel, and dwelling place, through it all.

Then I was fed up of just not being happy with my situation in England and thought of going to the states, but I am only going to say this once so that it doesn't look like a complaint, I just felt like some people didn't like me, so I just refrained was scared but no longer scared, but just refrained if it is meant to be, God will make a way for me to go there.

It can be a very scary journey and daunting very scary Journey being a vulnerable adult, know that because of unnatural sexual urges stimulated by a love potion:

- can lead strangers into your life, both those you would and might not usually go out with, leading you to do what God said you shouldn't do, *which is to not fornicate*, it is sad. Which can lead to your death eventually, do you know that man? SOMETIMES I THINK VULNER ABLE PEOPLE ARE BETTER OFF ON THEIR OWN OR AS NUNS. *On your own or as a nun the choice is yours.* That is, if a Mister right cannot come along, only because of this, then maybe you are better off alone I don't know, it's up to you though, I wouldn't settle for a relationship that I won't be happy in; and I am not talking about what the man looks like, I talking finding that special person that makes you happy, so take care.
- SEXUAL DESIRE CAN BE stimulated through touching the opposite sex.
- But can also be stimulated through aphrodisiac Viagra.

We all know education is important, if you despise it, it can lead to poverty. How are you supposed to learn something, if the teachers aren't motivating you to learn plus aren't teaching properly.

How will you know if the fault is coming from you because you are:

1. *1) Not really intelligent in the first place,*
2. *2) Or if it is because you aren't taught right in the first place.*
3. *Or Perhaps, maybe you are not very academic in the first instance*
    Then learn a trade or a craft.

If your right to defend for yourself is taken from you, I'm afraid you will not be able to afford the basic essential things in life. This is the issue we need to address.

Education is a seasonal exercise and training of your mind and capacity to get information, retain it and use it in a job, to improve society's needs.

So now we can see that the need to take teaching education seriously, is vital.

God put the teacher there to teach, so why don't they do their job.

Byeeeeeeee !

Pro 13:3 ;12-14 KJV

Pro 13:3 "He that keepeth his mouth keepeth his life: but he that openeth wide his lips shall have destruction." Basically, if you're not sure of how people will receive what you're about to say, maybe you shouldn't, say it then.

Pro 13:12 "Hope deferred maketh the heart sick: but when the desire cometh, it is a tree of life."

Pro 13:13 "Whoso despiseth the word shall be destroyed: but he that feareth the commandment shall be rewarded."

Pro 13:14 "The law of the wise is a fountain of life, to depart from the snares of death."

Pro 13:14 "The law of the wise is a fountain of life, <u>to depart from the snares of death.</u>"

Psalm 116:6-8
King James Version

6 The Lord preserveth the simple: I was brought low, and he helped me.

7 Return unto thy rest, O my soul; for the Lord hath dealt bountifully with thee.

8 <u>For thou hast delivered my soul from death, mine eyes from tears, and my feet from falling.</u>

I Cor 12 :25 "That there should be no schism in the body; but that the members should have the same care one for another."

All are important, stay in your place God has placed you. Everyone cannot be a queen, a king, a prince/ princess, a doctor or a lawyer, a pharmacist, so if people think you are not worthy, then that is their personal opinion!!!

Note when people use you, then start to look down on you like you are nothing, say to yourself you are something! What is their problem? Some people don't even have a job, you do and are complaining about people that don't have a job,....

.... Maybe some people should stay where God put them and leave people alone pls.

I feel like people try to make you feel stupid so that you can feel worthless so to stop what you are doing, so that they can replace you.

Good bye, God bless.

> 🕐 *No one has the power to know where you are going unless God tells them, Some can read minds because God gave them the power to do so.*

No one has the power to know where you are going unless God tells them, Some can read minds because *God gave them the power to do so*

Also, just because someone can read you mind, doesn't mean you have to say yes that it is true what you are thinking. You have the choice to decline their mind reading as your thoughts are personal good or bad.

You have the right to remain silent, as anything, good or bad, that you are thinking before you get to change your mind to be good, they can use it against you,

They don't have powers to know where you are going to Go, in order to set a trap for you. God will only send good people to you, not bad people, *so stop your foolishness and start obeying the voice of God.* You know the right thing to do and won't do it. The bible says, to him who knows the right thing to do and does not do it **to him it is a sin.**

They might not tell you what God said they should tell you, **but it is** against the law for someone to set a trap for you in the sight **of God.**

⏱ *Teaching our children of the world around them*

Teach *our* children about the creepy crawlies of life, take them to the animal zoo park. We are the parents and are responsible for looking after our children, if not society will try to corrupt them. *So, do not leave your children with the children of the devil monsters and strangers, like the creepy crawlies of this world,* they are creepy *can be* dangerous.

Let us pray for our children and bring them up in the way of the Lord, so that they will not be bullies like Cain towards Able, two children of our father in heaven.

1 Corinthians 15:33 King James Version

1Cor 15 :33 "Be not deceived: evil communications corrupt good manners."

Kjv Ecclesiates 10:8 "He that diggeth a pit shall fall into it; and whoso breaketh an hedge, a serpent shall bite him."

I'm notsaying don't go to other countries on holiday. But be careful, as you don't know the God they serve there; and what are the laws guiding animals there.

In my own opinion, Some serve oracles that are strange o -!!!-

Definition of oracle by google= "Greek history/ religion

1. "a priest or priestess acting as a medium, through whom advice or prophecy was sought from. The gods in classical antiquity."
2. "A response or message given by an oracle, especially an ambiguous one."

First of all these are all a guess.

Medical people lie about that men have to release sperm, though in actual fact, men don't have to release sperm until given medication to release in their partner.

Likewise, a woman is not supposed to use her period until given medication, so that she can get pregnant. This is a speculation a guess. So any form of IUS SHORT FOR INTRAUTERINE SYSTEM IN THE MEDICAL TERMs contraceptive wire or plastics coils, inserted in you or a sterilisation, a female having her fallopian tube tied or cut up, vasectomy, all of these acts are not necessary and are therefore evil from the pit of hell, sex lies and your soul, you'll be lucky if you survive the operation.

I think so. unless for crucial and serious medical reasons, I don't agree with these methods of contraceptives.

BUT Abortive PILLS ARE A PERSONAL CHOICE !!!

- *Medical people want to kill you, it's the same people who lie that you have to have (hair around a Female's private), or (hair around a male's private).*
- *The same medics, give you aphrodisiac and Viagra, so you can be exposed to contraceptives,*
- *the same people give a release of sperm and period at the wrong time, again so you can use contraceptives, that could endanger your life it could lead to your termination.*
- *The same people put you under the inf luence of Viagra / aphrodisiac so to lead you to promiscuity and possible sexually transmitted disease.*

These are the sort of lies, that can lead to death. Sex lies and your soul. Can a loving God instruct you about you life.

...... instead of instructing the Clergies men or women of God about your life issues? This is not to be rude, it's just a question.

<u>Christian songs</u>	<u>Christian songs</u> Continued
<u>1.</u> *Lanre – God blesses my family and my business;* Cece Winnans – He's a Wonder; Mercy said No; Never thirst again.	<u>15.</u> Let hope rise – Hillsong; All consuming fire you're my hearts desire & meditation- Kent Henry
<u>2.</u> *Tope Alabi – Egbega Egbega*	<u>16.</u> Consuming Fire-CFN
<u>3.</u> *Damita – I love you; it all belongs to you*	<u>17.</u> *Chris Martins CFN– He is God*
<u>4.</u> Hillsongs – In control;hope of the world, ocean deep;Lead me to the cross	<u>18.</u> *Mary Mary – somebody, shackles; Jesus culture-One thing remains; your love never fails*
<u>5.</u> *Sinach – Great are you Lord; The name of Jesus*	<u>19.</u> Lara Gergorge- Dansaki;
<u>6.</u> *Rebecca st james – Lamb of God, God of wonders beyond our galaxy*	<u>20.</u> Chris Tomlin- water you turned to wine; forever
<u>7.</u> *Mat Redman- Better is one day in your courts*	<u>21.</u> Don Moen- Thank you Lord
<u>8.</u> *Junita Bynum – Never thirst again*	<u>22.</u> Fred Hammond- I wanna be your; closer
<u>9.</u> *William Mcdowell- Won't go back to the way it was, I give myself away*	<u>23.</u> Casting Crown- Praise in the storm; Beth Croft – I stand in awe of you

<u>10.</u> *Joann Rosario- Holy God; Follow me; more than anything*	<u>24.</u> Amazing Love- no name found; More of you – sinach
<u>11.</u> Benjamin dube- *Bow down and worship him*	<u>25.</u> Kierra sheard- Indescribable
<u>12.</u> Kirk Franklin – The lamb of God	<u>26.</u> Tamela man-Take me to the king
<u>13.</u> Tasha Cobs – Fill me up	<u>27.</u> Paul Wilbur – Holy God
<u>14.</u> Chris Martins - he is God Hillsong - Here with you; River wild; oceans	<u>28.</u> <u>Itusile Nigerian musician;</u> Israel Houghton- Lord you are good and your mercies endureth forever "you'll Never thirst" – Anointed
<u>15.</u> Hillsongs: In control; Beneath the waters	29. Kari job -the more I seek you
	<u>30.</u> The News boys- God is not dead; Kofi Thompson Ghana- God you are good and your mercies endureth forever Praise in the storm – Casting crowns
	31. Beth Croft – I stand in awe of you

Hymns	Hymns continued
1. Showers of blessing;	8. Take my life and let it be
2. Shine Jesus shine; in Christ Alone	9. Immortal, invisible God
3. On Christ the solid Rock I stand	10. My faith has found a resting place
4. I count it all as loss	11. The steadfast Love of the Lord
5. King of Kings Majesty	12. *Amazing* Grace
6. It is well with my soul	13. Heaven came down and Glory filled my soul
7. Be still for the presence of the Lord is here	14. Shana Wilson- Press in your presence

<u>Baby names</u>

1. Femi; OlorunFemi
2. Gabriel; Gaby, <u>Grace, Ruth</u>
3. Emoji, feyikogbon- kgbon, Anna Hanna
4. Emojilet, Emojile, Emoan, <u>Emoanlet,</u> Emojilenorhmsil
5. Catelan; Benji
6. Benjisil; cole
7. Dathan; Benjianlet, Benjianle, Dathan, Dathaniel
8. annaneels; Lomi (lomi-lomi)
9. coleneels ; loammi
10. Adana, Adani, <u>Benjianle, Benjianlenorhmsil</u>
11. Moona, Mooni, Aphaxada
12. Joseph, Josephine
13. Joy, Joyce, Adedayo
14. <u>Adeniyi, Adebola</u>
15. <u>Olu</u>
16. <u>Neels</u>
17. <u>Michael, Michaellet</u>

In conclusion, I reiterate and repeat, I want you to be aware of something, I used to get angry at God for my mishaps /mistakes made in life, bad decisions, though I am now not angry at God for the temptations I face, neither am I saying that God is bad, but I am just trying to make a way of escape if you like out of a difficult situation. Also, trying to make a way to manage temptations as a believer or as an infidel- a non believer of Christ. Remember God is sovereign, and he makes things perfect in his own time.

I will bless the God who gives and takes away.

Also, I'd like to say this, in my own personal opinion, I feel that some witch Drs are reasonable people, meaning that they do what they feel is right for them. I believe that everyone has a freedom of right to express what they believe in, <u>as long as it has nothing to do with harming, others nor me personally or don't try their magic on me.</u>

I may not believe in what they practice, but it is their right <u>to practice it in some countries.</u>

However, I want you to note that, I don't believe all witch Drs practice voodoo. But the ones, <u>alongside ordinary people,</u> who do practice voodoo, are harmful and can destroy people's lives, Sex lies and your soul.

To be honest, I never want to have anything to do with these kind of people, or have any form of contact with such people in my life.

Also I am not saying having sexual intercourse is wrong, but what I am saying is try not to fornicate to be having sex outside wedlock. Or if you will do this, then avoid sleeping around. If you can't help to fornicate maybe because you suspect you are under the inf luence of Viagra or aphrodisiac, then make sure you protect yourself, let the man get tested.

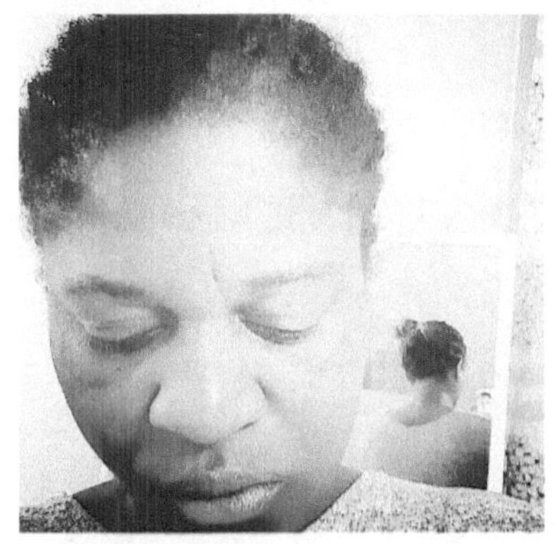

Lastly note, when you go for a blood test, ask for the appropriate needle, a butterf ly needle, as I have had experiences, where the nurses have been nasty, and they don't carry out the blood test in a good way, you end up bruised, to discourage you doing the test the next time. This is wrong, they know that they have made you sexually active !!!

It's like the devil is after your soul at all cost, it starts with silly little banter / jokes, so don't lose your focus at the end of the day. Yes, I will die one day, but not like this, not through lies and manipulations.

Sex, lies and your Soul. As if life is not complicated enough as it is. Good day. Peace and Love.

Ruth 1:20
King James Version

[20] And she said unto them, Call me not Naomi, call me Mara: for the Almighty hath dealt very bitterly with me.

Psalm 23:5-6
King James Version

[5] Thou preparest a table before me in the presence of mine enemies: thou anointest my head with oil; my cup runneth over.

[6] Surely goodness and mercy shall follow me all the days of my life: and I will dwell in the house of the LORD for ever.

Psalm 118:29
King James Version

29 "O give thanks unto the LORD; for he is good: for his mercy endureth for ever."

Though like Naomi, situations in our lives may makes us think that God doesn't love us anymore. But I've come to tell you a good news. That no matter what your vulnerability is, God can still show up to turn things around. If we have a faith as small as a mustard seed, you, believe in yourself and in the power in the name of Jesus.

So then, I pray that all bitter situations in our lives, turn to sweetness in the mighty name of Jesus.

God has a plan for our lives no matter our condition. If only you will believe, but be careful that you are aware, that there are evil people are around and that no matter the condition good or bad, God will send help.

But, note you have to do your part, by staying in tune and in line with God's plan for your life. Also, this is why, we should always be connected to hear from God about our lives.

This is why you need to give your life to Jesus, be born again, also to have a rapport with a good man of God or a male or female clergy.

<u>WE ALL PRAY FOR longevity OF LIFE, in ChristJesus' name, who is our Lord and personal saviour.</u>

Everyone testifies of the goodness of God; and that God is good plus his mercies endures forever.

<u>Song</u>

I have seen the Lord's goodness, his mercies and compassions.

I have seen the Lord's goodness, Hallelujah praise the Lord.

O Lord you have been so good, you are so good to me, O Lord you are excellent in my life every day.

O Lord you have been so good, you are so good to me, O Lord you are excellent in my life!

A song

I praise you I praise you O lord (2X)

In my life, I see what you're doing, one more time I lift my voice in Praise of your name, I lift my voice in praise of your name.

This year or the year to come, I pray that God may grant me my dreams to learn new things etc. etc. If it happens it happens, if it doesn't it doesn't, either way, let the will of God be done.

Also, to keep trusting him and other things.

www.ingramcontent.com/pod-product-compliance
Lightning Source LLC
Chambersburg PA
CBHW051448250726
48655CB00001B/310